PRAISE FOR FLIRTING
WITH DARKNESS

"Ben Courson is a young and much-needed voice for today's generation. His youthful energy is matched by his penetrating scriptural insights. This is all on display in his new book, *Flirting with Darkness*. Ben takes the topic of depression head-on and gives biblical insight on how to defeat it."

Greg Laurie,
bestselling author, radio and TV personality, and founder of Harvest Crusades

"Ben Courson is one of the most inspiring speakers I have ever had the joy of getting to know. His love for life and message of faith shine out of him like the rays of the sun. Just being around Ben makes me feel good, and his message will make *you* feel good too."

Debbie Matenopoulos,
two-time Emmy Award–nominated television host of
Hallmark's *Home and Family* and ABC's *The View*

"In *Flirting with Darkness*, Ben shows that the black keys of wistfulness and sorrow can make music every bit as beautiful as the white keys. If life feels like a song and you've forgotten the tune, these pages will train your ears to hear heaven's music once again."

Jeremy Camp,
Gold-charting singer and subject of the movie *I Still Believe*

"Ben Courson is a voice for our generation. A poet and preacher with a powerful message of new life in Jesus! We believe his new book, *Flirting with Darkness*, is going to encourage the world to look to Jesus, our only hope in this uncertain time."

Rich and DawnCheré Wilkerson,
pastors of Vous Church and stars of reality TV show *Rich in Faith*

"Stress, depression, and anxiety are silent killers. Thank you, Ben, for tackling this dark but real topic, and for providing hope to a hopeless generation."

Kellin Quinn,
lead singer of Sleeping with Sirens

We compete not for earthly trophies but for heavenly crowns, and my friend Ben wrote this book to help the injured heal up and obtain spiritual victories. *Flirting with Darkness* is a playbook that will equip downcast souls to play offense and defeat depression!"

Randall Cunningham,
Philadelphia Eagles Hall of Fame quarterback

"*Flirting with Darkness* moved me with its vulnerability and its unveiling of the world of comparison we live in each day. I can't wait to see how Ben's book will change people by stirring faith and hope within."

Brennley Brown,
actress and country music star on NBC's *The Voice*

"Dark days are inevitable. Whether you've experienced it yet or not, life is uncertain and you never know when tragedy will knock. That is why this book is not only an encouraging resource but a vital weapon. With depth and clarity, Ben draws on his personal experience to offer you the practical tools and the courage you need to retaliate against the weight of darkness and walk forward in freedom."

Levi Lusko,
pastor and bestselling author

"*Flirting with Darkness* shines a much-needed light on the epidemic of depression in today's generation and how we can find victory over it!"

Meredith Foster,
author, YouTube and Instagram celebrity

"In *Flirting with Darkness* I found new weapons to slay the persistent darkness of depression and conquer it for good. I will forever choose to 'dance in the light.' Thank you, Ben! You are saving lives."

Myrka Dellanos,
Emmy Award–winning TV star

"Ben's colorful and passionate ability to tell the truth sells the truth. Many people are talking about living with depression, but Ben has taken the stance of actually defeating it. I am so blessed by the message of hope in this book."

Doe Jones,
three-time Grammy-nominated singer

"Ben Courson's pen is one of the freshest around these days. In this book he tackles one of life's toughest subjects, and he tackles it head-on! Ben invites you to go on a journey—to climb into the soul of one who suffers with depression and climb out the other side into a brightened, hope-filled world. *Flirting with Darkness* is packed with powerful examples that bring God's plan for your life into bold relief."

Skip Heitzig,
pastor and bestselling author

"Who knew that a book about such a sobering subject could be so spiritually informative and enjoyable to read? If you struggle with depression or thoughts of suicide, this was written just for you."

Matt Crouch,
president of TBN

"Ben Courson is an awesome example of God's light on Earth."

Patricia Lovely,
actress on the Oprah Winfrey Network

"Ben Courson is a courageous man who fought depression on the frontlines of the battle and came back victorious. In *Flirting with Darkness*, Ben unveils the divine resources, spiritual weapons, and battle-tested tactics that lead one out of the dark valleys of depression and into the light."

Chad Williams,
Navy SEAL and author of *SEAL of God*

"Ben's courage to tackle topics that most struggle with but few are willing to speak on is inspiring. Be encouraged as you build your faith through this read!"

Beaver Fleming,
professional skateboarder

"Ben's God-given ability to use Scripture to encourage people is extraordinary."

Beneil Dariush,
world-ranked MMA fighter and UFC Champion

"It's no secret that anxiety and depression are two of today's biggest yet hidden epidemics. Ben's careful but thorough approach is not only important but necessary."

Jordan Doww,
actor, comedian, and Teen Choice Award finalist

"The millennial generation has found a voice of hope in *Flirting with Darkness*. I highly encourage you to read this book and to pass it on to others. It just might save a life—even yours."

Jack Hibbs,
pastor and radio personality

"*Flirting with Darkness* epitomizes true hope! It gives us key tools we all need."

Jason McCarthy,
professional English soccer star

"Ben Courson is one of the most encouraging and positive people you will ever meet! He knows exactly what it takes to beat depression and come out on top."

Taylor Kalupa,
star of ABC's *The Fix*

"I'm always excited to read and listen to anything Ben is working on! He has walked a journey that has given him a genuine sensitivity and perspective for life."

Ryan Stevenson,
Grammy-nominated singer

"*Flirting with Darkness* isn't merely a manual on overcoming depression; it's a manifesto! Ben Courson's personal vulnerability will shine a light in the deepest pits of depression and help many climb out."–

Bianca Juarez Olthoff,
bestselling author and church planter

"Ben's ability to articulate the tools necessary to fight depression is amazing. *Flirting with Darkness* serves as a beacon of light for anyone struggling with the darkness of this world!"

Cody Flom,
professional scooter rider

"Ben Courson is one of the most fascinating and transformational young leaders around. *Flirting with Darkness* dives into depression and gives us the biblical tools we need to combat it. At a time when so many people are losing their lives to suicide, this is a book our culture desperately needs."

Billy Hallowell,
journalist and contributor to the *Washington Post*, FoxNews.com,
and the *Huffington Post*

"Using the Bible and history, science and neurobiology, *Flirting with Darkness* attacks depression with a vengeance and offers heavenly hope!"

Rich Wilkerson Sr.,
pastor and author

"Ben's message of joy in the Lord and hope's triumph in all circumstances is encouraging and contagious! He inspires us all to never give up, dream big, and know that God will always be faithful."

Joey Buran,
Hall of Fame pro surfer and Olympic coach

"He's done it again! Ben Courson is built to be a weapon of hope. If you're looking for a friend to help you escape the hole of despair you may have found yourself in, *read this book*! Your life will be changed!"

Austin French,
NBC's Rising Star

"I'm so thankful to Ben for writing *Flirting with Darkness*. He understands emptiness. Despair. Palpable darkness. Yet he also gets what it means to not throw in the towel. To fight. To persevere. And to hope Godward. If you feel like you are drowning, let this soul-rescuer throw you a life vest and offer you some good old-fashioned hope."

Bobby Conway,
founder of the One Minute Apologist

"As you read Ben's new book, the light of Christ will shine through whatever darkness you are facing, and hope will fill your soul."

Ashley Key,
CBN News

"Ben Courson has the ear of a young generation, but they aren't the only ones who need to hear this important message."

David Guzik,
author of *The David Guzik Bible Commentary*

"I have never felt so safe and warm at one time."

Jamie Miller,
star of *The Voice UK*

"*Flirting with Darkness* holds a timely and timeless message for those lacking hope. If you or your loved one struggles with depression, this is a book for you!"

Bobby Schuller,
TV host of *Hour of Power*

"*Flirting with Darkness* is captivating, and it will lure you in with authenticity, humor, and wisdom. Ben isn't afraid to be brave and resilient, and he says what needs to be said."

Christina Eileen,
TikTok star

"If you need some refreshment and hope today, picking up *Flirting with Darkness* will be the right choice."

Steven Bancarz,
bestselling author

"It's about time for Christians to speak up about depression. In *Flirting with Darkness*, Ben leads the way in this necessary conversation, bravely sharing his story of moving from darkness to light and offering hope that depression doesn't have to have the final word. His story will touch you and his courage will inspire you."

Debra Fileta,
author and licensed counselor

"*Flirting with Darkness* not only accounts for the marvelous testimony of God's power and promises in Ben's life, but also foreshadows the glorious freedom that awaits you as well."

Kirby Minnick,
YouTube and podcast star

"Ben is one of the great wordsmiths and thinkers of our generation, and in this powerful and important new book he tackles what has tragically become an epidemic in our generation. Ben is a hope dealer, but he has also battled the darkness, and so his hope comes from the gritty place that makes him a trusted guide in the struggle."

Matt Brown,
evangelist and author

"Ben is living proof that our God takes us through valleys, up on mountaintops, and back down again, just to use what we learn during both for His glory."

Austin Carlile,
lead singer of Attack Attack! and Of Mice and Men

"This book is a game changer! We don't have to live with depression, and *Flirting with Darkness* shows you exactly how that is possible."

David Nurse,
author and NBA shooting coach

"Both courageous and gentle."

Scott Gaunson,
YouTube star of *How Ridiculous*

"*Flirting with Darkness* is rich with both defeat and triumph. It'll give hope to your journey."

Grant Skeldon,
author featured in the *Wall Street Journal*

"Reading *Flirting with Darkness* feels like sitting in on a therapy session between Ben and his psychologist, or, better yet, God himself. Ben is a fresh voice for a lost and hurting world because he has been there, lost and hurt, and found hope, The Hope, and so can you."

Stephen Christian,
lead singer of Anberlin

"We live in a world that is increasingly competitive and comparative, where people can often feel inadequate and full of despair, where some even consider taking matters into their own hands and putting an end to their suffering. Here is a book reminding us that God is sovereign and loving—in complete control—no matter our circumstances."

Samuel Smadja,
Israeli TV host and pastor

"This book is a guide and a friend to those who have been or are in the valley-low."

Thane Marcus Ringler,
professional golfer

"Get ready to have your mind blown! Deep calls to deep—that's the best way I can describe Ben's fascinating teachings in *Flirting with Darkness*. He's done it again!"

Cambria Joy,
author and YouTube star

"Ben Courson's honesty is disarming. His story is compelling. And his insights are deep. Take this journey with him. Stop flirting with darkness and join Ben in the light!"

Daniel Fusco,
pastor, author, and TV personality

"If I didn't have someone like Ben to help me get through the lows in my life, I would not have been able to have the success I have had."

Brady Breeze,
Rose Bowl Defensive MVP, *USA TODAY* All-Bowl Team

"Ben Courson offers an elegant solution to the suicidal trends facing Gen Z. Ben's style of communication balances playfulness and pastoral care, addressing the topic of depression from a youthful, gospel-centered neurotheology that will make you laugh, think, and worship the God of hope he knows so well."

Brooks Gibbs, PhD,
psychologist

"Ben's book is full of history, facts, and hidden gems from the Bible. You won't want to stop reading!"

Alex Samuel,
professional soccer Player of the Year

"A way forward through the darkness."

Chas Smith,
journalist for *Surfing Magazine*

"*Flirting with Darkness* reaches into the souls of those struggling with depression. Ben reminds us that even in the darkest shadows, God is enthroned on our storms. A story the world needs to hear."

Brittany Dawn Brannon Kennada,
Miss Arizona USA

FLIRTING

WITH

DARKNESS

BEN COURSON

HARVEST HOUSE PUBLISHERS
EUGENE, OREGON

Cover design by Faceout Studio

Cover photo © Marzz Studio / Shutterstock

Interior design by KUHN Design Group

For bulk, special sales, or ministry purchases, please call 1-800-547-8979. Email: Customerservice@hhpbooks.com

This book studies depression through the lenses of personal story, history, science, and the Bible. The information presented herein is meant to be used for general resource purpose only. It is not intended as specific mental health medical advice for any individual and should not substitute medical advice from a health care professional. If you have or think you may have a medical problem, speak to your doctor or health care practitioner immediately about your risk and possible treatments. Do not engage in any therapy or treatment without consulting a medical professional.

Flirting with Darkness

Copyright © 2020 by Ben Courson

Published by Harvest House Publishers

Eugene, Oregon 97408

www.harvesthousepublishers.com

ISBN 978-0-7369-7890-3 (pbk.)

ISBN 978-0-7369-7891-0 (eBook)

ISBN 978-0-7369-8337-2 (eAudio)

Library of Congress Cataloging-in-Publication Data

Names: Courson, Ben, - author.

Title: Flirting with darkness / Ben Courson.

Description: Eugene : Harvest House Publishers, 2020.

Identifiers: LCCN 2020012284 (print) | LCCN 2020012285 (ebook) | ISBN 9780736978903 (trade paperback) | ISBN 9780736978910 (ebook)

Subjects: LCSH: Depression, Mental--Religious aspects--Christianity. | Depressed persons--Religious life. | Courson, Ben,

Classification: LCC BV4910.34 .C68 2020 (print) | LCC BV4910.34 (ebook) | DDC 248.8/625--dc23

LC record available at https://lccn.loc.gov/2020012284

LC ebook record available at https://lccn.loc.gov/2020012285

Printed in the United States of America

20 21 22 23 24 25 26 27 28 / BP-SK / 10 9 8 7 6 5 4 3 2 1

CONTENTS

PART ONE:
FLIRTING WITH DARKNESS

PART TWO:
DEFEATING DEPRESSION

PART THREE:
DANCING IN THE LIGHT

This book is dedicated to three women who found me in my darkest depression and loved me back into the light:

my sisters Mare Bear and Christy,

and my mom, Tambo—the most hopeful person I've ever known

WHY I WROTE
THIS BOOK

Every 40 seconds, somewhere in the world, someone will kill themselves.

There are 123 suicides each day in the United States. In fact, there are twice as many suicides as murders.

And, sadly, suicide is the second leading cause of death in the world for those aged 15-24.

It has become an epidemic in our time, especially among the younger generation.

That is why I wrote this book.

Suicide. Must. Stop.

((((( )))))

For many people, the temptation of suicide arises out of a deep depression. So this book is devoted to defeating depression. I know it's hipster to say, "I've learned to live with depression," but I want to argue that we are not called to live with depression but to defeat it.

I want to begin this book the same way the Bible begins, with a picture of how God intends things to be. We are created to be kings destined to rule in God's kingdom, not slaves cowering to the dark lord of depression. Genesis 1:27 tells us we are created in the "image of God," and in the Hebrew language that phrase is *selem Elohim*.[1] All over the ancient Near East, this was the title given to kings. For example, the pharaoh who was called Amon-Re had a name that meant "the image of the sun god." All over Mesopotamia, the king was nicknamed for the god of that nation. The king was not only a ruler over all the land but also a high priest who mediated blessing to his kingdom.

So, if God decrees that *we* are kings and priests (Revelation 1:6), then it means we are to have dominion over the earth and subdue it, not live lives of those subjugated and defeated.

As someone who once journeyed quite a distance down the long, dark tunnel of depression and faced the temptation of suicide, I can assure you that *suicide is not the answer*. In fact, it's just the opposite. I believe no one *has* to live with the kind of deep depression that once stifled my happiness and contentment.

At its root, the answer to depression is a renewed hope, and my number one goal in this book is to help you find that hope.

Frankly, I'm all about hope.

The title of my last book was *Optimisfits*, a word of my own invention that is a kind of collision between the words *optimistic* and *misfit*. In my personal, made-up dictionary, the definition of an optimisfit is as follows: "a nonconformist; an adventurer; a person who lives with childlike wonder, wild abandon, and unapologetic optimism." This attitude is the best way of defeating depression in your life. Those of us who have embraced the identity of being an optimisfit proudly wear another label: rebels of hope.

We are rebelling against the kind of conformity and negativity that make up the zeitgeist of despair in our culture. We refuse to fit into that system. Because it is killing us. Literally. We're going to look at depression through the lenses of personal story, the Bible, history, and science. They have all led me to one conclusion: You don't have to settle for just learning to *live with* your depression. You don't have to accept it as a character trait of your personality. No, you can rise above it!

This new outlook made all the difference for me.

It helped me climb up out of the deep well of my own despair and disappointment and breathe the fresh, pure air of renewed hope.

It can do the same for you.

PART ONE

FLIRTING

WITH

DARKNESS

CONFESSIONS
OF AN EX-SUICIDE

Let me start with a confession: I am an ex-suicide.

By that I mean I was strongly tempted to take my own life. I stared the possibility of suicide directly in the face, but in the end I walked away without having done the deed.

There was a time, though, when such an outcome was not at all assured.

Nearly 800,000 people worldwide die by their own hand every year. I was almost a statistic.

Sometime in my mid-twenties, I made a careful evaluation of my life, and I felt categorically doomed. So, I did what any "sensible" millennial would do. I pulled a large knife from a kitchen drawer so that I could use it to kill myself. Frankly, I thought it would hurt less to put an end to my life than to endure the continuous scorpion stings of despair that had become my daily bread.

I'd already done all the classic things suicidal chaps are known for. I Googled to find the most effective methods of how one could go about the inelegant business of offing oneself. I pondered many different scenarios. At night I would sometimes sneak up to the top of the tallest buildings in the city and walk around the exposed edge—a makeshift version of a lethal tightrope. I once terrified an unsuspecting security guard, who, it turns out, was watching me. In my flirtation with the grim reaper, I put myself in other scary situations and wondered what it would feel like to end it all as I ventured out onto the brink of death. I raced around town at seriously excessive speeds on a rocket motorcycle without either a helmet or a license or any knowledge of how to ride the fool thing. The simplest mistake would have drawn down the curtain on my existence.

I guess you could say I was actively courting death. I was like Albert Camus, a famous philosopher and novelist who decided that life was absurd...and therefore not worth investing much effort in to protect. He allowed himself to be a passenger with a notoriously reckless driver and ended up dead at a young age in a car accident. For a time, I found significant appeal in somehow being a passive victim like Camus rather than taking matters into my own hands.

Fortunately, and perhaps undeservedly, I didn't fall victim to any of my foolhardy predispositions.

My guardian angel was obviously working a double shift.

(((( ))))

Does recounting these stories about my flirtation with darkness sound as though I'm composing the dramatic lyrics to an emo song or penning an overly sensationalized melodrama?

Yes, I get it. Those of my readers who are a little older had parents in World War II or Vietnam and lived through stuff like the Cuban Missile Crisis, the cultural war between the hippies and the Nixon fans, or watched dumbfounded as the twin towers collapsed on September 11. They might cast a wry smile at my intensely dramatic personal angst.

They have been through a lot, and compared with such horrors, what are the problems of my generation?

Here we millennials are, lounging in Mom's basement eating Sour Patch Kids and playing endless games of Fortnite. We live with all the comforts of life, and yet we are unhappy, unhappy, unhappy. And some of us sometimes just want to die.

Though our rampant epidemic of depression might strike earlier generations as ridiculous and self-obsessed, it isn't. To us, the pain is all too real.

Even if you live in a run-down trailer park, suffering from downward mobility and economic hardship, you still live better than the kings of old. Once, I skated into a homeless camp where they were watching Netflix in their tents. Need I say more? We have creature comforts and amenities that earlier generations could only dream of. Still, Generation Why is depressed, and no one seems to know the reason.

((((( )))))

One of the ancient Hebrew writers of the book of Proverbs understood exactly what I am talking about. Proverbs 18:14 spells out his perspective in all its raw power: a man's spirit can sustain him in sickness, but who can bear a broken spirit?

That phrase—*a broken spirit*—defined my struggle with depression and my flirtation with suicide better than anything else I'd ever heard. I'd reached a place where my spirit was just broken. Crushed, shattered, and battered was exactly how I had come to feel.

This was the result of a history of heartbreaks. I was recently diagnosed with complex PTSD (post-traumatic stress disorder) related to all the things I went through. My counselor confessed to me that I've had one of the most difficult depressions she's ever had to deal with. It takes time to get past the hard stuff.

I felt like the martyr George Eagles, who lived and died in Queen Mary's day. Because of his great pains from traveling from place to place to "confirm the brethren," he was nicknamed "Trudge Over the World." This name fit me like a glove, jumping from airplane to airplane with a depleted immune system and ending up exhausted, burntout, and depressed.

(((( ))))

I've witnessed and experienced my fair share of tragedy in my life.

One of my sisters died in a car crash when I was just a kid. I remember being pulled out of class by the principal and was dumb enough to think it meant my family was going to throw me a surprise party. Instead, I came home to find my family weeping over how Jessica had been killed in an accident. Before the accident she'd been joking that she'd always be single because Dad had told her she could only date someone who was godlier than her. "I'm the godliest person I know," she had said with a wink. And the next day, as we mourned her death, my brother commented that now she had found her man. She'd become a bride of Christ. Losing her remains the dominant memory of my childhood.

My dad's first wife also died in a car wreck.

My brother, who struggled for years with sickness from a brain tumor, Crohn's disease, and cancer, recently joined his mom and my sister in eternity. My family knows something about living in the shadow of death.

Then I was blindsided by heartbreak when a relationship I'd been in for eight years ended in tragedy, leaving me shattered and confused and broken. I shook convulsively and sobbed my eyes out. In the days that followed I felt hollow inside—the prelude to months and months of total emotional shutdown when I felt nothing at all, becoming so numb that I was like a robot with dead batteries.

All that is going to leave a mark.

The devastating result of these tragedies was the accumulating slow torment of ten years of chronic depression. It felt like death by a thousand pinpricks or the continual dripping of Chinese water torture. Drip. Drip. Drip. An unending succession of droplets that wore away my self-image and self-confidence and my trust in God. It left me begging for death.

A broken spirit indeed.

((((( )))))

There is no other emotional experience quite like depression. You are worn down by the inability to riddle out some sense in life as the gathering dark engulfs you with all manner of existential terrors.

Maybe, you begin to think, the universe is not a hospitable place for you.

All the things you really cared about seem out of reach or meaningless.

And you feel dead inside.

So, I had all the predictable responses.

I spent time staring at the walls.

I read Sylvia Plath. (Spoiler alert: She stuck her head in an oven. Happy trails…)

I drew the blinds and sat in darkness.

I made a music mix called "Laments."

And I seriously considered killing myself.

Then something happened…and this book tells that story…

SQUIRT GUN DRIVE-BYS AND FUNERAL DIRECTORS

I didn't always struggle with depression. But it is amazing how quickly things can turn around in your life.

Most of my high school years felt like one giant, never-ending party. I was like Tigger. Bouncy, bouncy, fun, fun, fun. My life made sense to me, and I was enjoying every minute of it, even if there had been some dark events in my past. If someone had asked me then to describe what life felt like, I might have used a phrase like "robustly flavored donuts of fun." I wasn't dealing with any major existential crises or struggles with the Big Questions about meaning and purpose. I was fine with loving God and having a good time. That was my recipe for life.

I met all of the goals I set for myself in high school. I won the homecoming crown and was the student body president. I was selected for the All-League basketball squad and was one of the leading scorers in Orange County. I was soaring high.

I had crazy friends, most of them almost as nutty as me.

Because our school was near Disneyland, my friends and I practically lived there. When we were bored with the rides, we invented other ways to let craziness reign in the Magic Kingdom. We climbed up above the entrance to the Indiana Jones ride and dropped leaves and twigs down on unsuspecting guests waiting in line and anticipated their shocked response. During the nightly fireworks show, we would scream out at the top of our voices, "We're under attack," and make like we were taking cover. We were frequently chased by the security guards for our juvenile stunts, but they never caught us. If they had, we might still be locked in a cell with the pirates of the Caribbean!

Other times we'd pretend to be mountain climbers and scale the 30-foot storage shelves at our local IKEA store. Or we'd dress in neon pink short shorts and violently flail about (what we were doing hardly deserved to be called *dancing*) at the screamo shows we would attend. We engaged in drive-by shootings with our water pistols, and once we ended up in a literal car chase when someone took umbrage at being drenched. We even snuck into a corporate recycling center so we could do somersaults in the foam pits, and we climbed a fence to make use of the outdoor hot tubs at a five-star hotel.

Some of these activities were definitely irresponsible. Maybe a little stupid. But we weren't harming anyone. It was all pretty tame. And it was fun.

Christians gone wild!

Once a week hundreds of people crowded into my parents' home for the Bible study I was leading. My dad was a successful pastor, and I'd followed in his footsteps. By third grade, I had my first experience of preaching. By the time I was 16, I was traveling to other churches to share with their kids…and sometimes even with the adults. I was the happy kid on *Mission Possible*.

(((( ))))

I left high school early so I could train for the ministry. (A phrase which now gives me a case of the dry heaves…) I officially became a pastor during my senior year.

On the outside, everything looked great.

On the inside, I was struggling. I felt as if my future had been predetermined and I didn't have much choice. I was doing everything everyone expected of me, but I was growing cold and shriveled inside. I started feeling dead in my heart and soul, going through the motions without the emotions. It was a poor excuse for a life.

One day I was reading C.S. Lewis's book *A Grief Observed*. I had the stark realization as I browsed its pages that, like him, I had lost someone important to me—well, actually, several someones. And to top it all off, even more shocking, I realized I had lost myself. I realized I wasn't just unhappy—I was seriously and deeply depressed. I couldn't even figure out the right questions to ask. Like Mr. Lewis, I found myself inquiring about the shape of yellow.[1]

I was still acting like Pollyanna on the outside, but inside I felt more like Puddleglum.

The horrors began to howl inside my head.

(((( ))))

I wondered if becoming a pastor was the right move for me. I was allergic to the sameness and tameness of much of modern Churchianity. I knew I could never fit inside that box of expectations. And, honestly, I didn't even want to.

I felt like David when he faced Goliath. The giant's armor is described in detail (1 Samuel 17:4-7) because the Philistines possessed a type of metal previously unknown to the Hebrews, and their overall military technology was far ahead of them. In response, King Saul put his own armor on David. But it didn't fit. It was nearly impossible to move around. The armor slowed David down and actually made him more vulnerable to defeat. Only when he pulled it off and cast it aside could he stand face-to-face against the giant (verses 38-39).

Interestingly, the Bible tells us of some of the relatives of Saul who were ambidextrous slingers and expert archers (1 Chronicles 12:1-2 NKJV). Back then, deft slingshot-marksmen were as lethal as snipers. So, contrary to popular belief, when David cast off his armor to use a sling, he actually had a military advantage over Goliath! I needed to cast off my armor and play to my strengths if I was going to face my own Goliaths.

But it took me a while to figure that out. Instead, I tried ever harder to fit into the mold. I believed I needed to be super serious, super somber, and super saintly if I was going to succeed as a pastor. Many of the people I knew who were "in ministry" were fine chaps, but they looked as if they were employed and deployed by the local morgue. That just wasn't me. I was still the squirt gun–toting, raucous, rowdy, theme-park provocateur—a guy who would like nothing more than the opportunity to drive my Jeep into rivers just because I could.

I began to become convinced that professional ministry wasn't my vibe. I agreed with the great Supreme Court justice Oliver Wendell Holmes, who famously claimed that he might have become a minister if all the clergymen he knew hadn't acted like undertakers. So many of the pastors I knew, God bless 'em, gave funeral directors a run for their money when it came to their dimly lit sanctuaries and their ponderous organ-driven songs about how "this world has nothing for me" and the like.

((((( )))))

Julian the Apostate was a Roman emperor who tried to undo the work of his uncle Constantine, who had embraced Christianity and fought under the sign of the cross. Julian decided to reintroduce the pagan gods into Roman culture. Why? Because he believed Christianity made the Roman Empire weak. As William Barclay notes, he believed Christians were "pale-faced" and "flat-breasted"…and that even if the sun shone for them, they never saw it.[2] Of course, I'd never endorse

Julian's program, but when it came to how many of the Christians I knew behaved, I had to admit he had a point.

The great British social critic John Ruskin remembers playing with a set of jacks when he was a child, only to be rebuked by his pious aunt who told him that Christians weren't allowed to play with toys.[3] One wonders what long-term damage that did to his psyche...

This weak-kneed and legalistic Christianity was what I saw so many well-intentioned believers peddling. Their focus was on being "holy," which seemed to be a synonym for "miserable." I pursued this path with intensity, praying until the veins in my neck bulged or lying on my face, prostrate before a "holy" God. I tried to live up to the example of St. James, who was nicknamed "Old Camel Knees."

I devoured the most stringent writings of the Puritans.

One way or the other, I told myself, I was going to be one of these passionate God-fearers.

In my earlier book I referred to my squad and myself as optimisfits. But so many of the people I knew in ministry were more like pessimisfits. They seemed to fulfill the words of poet Algernon Swinburne, who once wrote, "Thou hast conquered, O pale Galilean; the world has grown gray from thy breath."[4]

I was struggling and unhappy and becoming ever more depressed. Those early days in ministry were as colorless as the opening scenes of *The Wizard of Oz*.

((((( )))))

My dream was to give a splash of hope and a dash of color to this world, but I found myself becoming an old soul in a young body—and not in a good way. I grew jaded and cynical, and I talked so much about "sinners in the hands of an angry God" that even Jonathan Edwards himself might have told me to lighten up![5]

I was becoming "religious" but not more like Jesus. I was becoming a Pharisee. I was defining myself by how much I had "given up for God." And I assumed that the more miserable I felt, the more holy I was becoming.

THE SHORTEST
VERSE IN THE BIBLE

Which Scripture verse best described my idea of the Christian ideal? How about the verse commonly pointed to as the shortest verse in the Bible:

"Jesus wept" (John 11:35).

Well, if I may interject a bit of biblical trivia here, it was pointed out to me by my friend Levi Lusko that John 11:35 is technically *not* the shortest verse in the Bible, despite the fact that everyone says it is. In fact, in the original Greek language in which the New Testament was written, that verse contains 16 characters.

There is actually a verse that is shorter, containing a mere 14 characters in the original language. It's Paul's admonition to "Rejoice always" (1 Thessalonians 5:16).

Perhaps, I began to believe, this is a much better ideal for my life. As Scripture says, "Weeping may stay for the night, but rejoicing comes in the morning" (Psalm 30:5).

That *morning* kind of faith is so much better than a *mourning* kind of faith!

(((( )))))

So, there I was, struggling to prove myself to God and others, and feeling like a charlatan.

Because I was at a loss for what I should be doing with my life, I went in search of a sunbeam. I studied books I had previously deemed to be dangerous or taboo, I poured out my heart to God in complete honesty, and I began to meet people who were more like the person I was actually created to be. I discovered there was an alternative way of "being a Christian" than making an agony out of my faith, and that the point of life was not to become more pious, but to become a friend of the God of hope, which is the apostle Paul's nickname for the great Creator God (Romans 15:13).

In the process I found a new focus and polestar toward which all my theology could gravitate: sacred optimism. Everybody was always talking about the cross, but I discovered that the early Christians in the book of Acts were every bit as focused on the resurrection. Perhaps that is why images of the cross are such a rare occurrence in early Christian art, and images and symbols of resurrection are so abundant! It wasn't until the early Middle Ages that the cross became a focus of art, which may say something important about what the early believers were focusing upon.

I saw that I needed to write myself into a narrative that ended with the empty tomb rather than pausing the movie in the middle of the passion of Christ.

It didn't happen overnight, but as I pursued this path my depression began to ease. It started to relax its iron grip on me as I began to see my life and my faith in a new way. The new narrative for my life was not a pious religious task, but a breathtaking adventure with the God of hope.

I started down a path that brought healing to my broken heart and gave my life a brand-new lens.

I learned a lot of things that helped me along the way, but now I was on a better journey. I followed the wizard into the hero's journey and wondered what surprises might lie in wait.

((((( )))))

I started taking long walks with God where I would tell Him about my dreams. Interestingly, scientific research has discovered that talking with God about your hopes, fears, and dreams has the same effect on your brain as years of therapy. So, I got vulnerable and opened up to Him. I decided to forgo all my attempts to live up to other people's expectations for my life and just be content with being who He had made me to be.

Paradoxically, I ended up working even harder, but now with a new attitude. I had a new outlook, a new focus, and a new sense of hope. This made all the hard work I was doing fun.

Having read that it takes an investment of 10,000 hours to excel at anything, I decided to invest 11,073 hours over the course of five years to become proficient at crafting a new way to write and teach. (Yes, I actually used stopwatches and timers, which is evidence of just how OCD I really am.) On the side I even wrote a fantasy trilogy just for the fun of it.

I started making room for new friends in my life, people with whom I undertook all kinds of crazy adventures.

I focused on creating a dreamality by doing the work that needed to be done. No more time riding the pine. I was in the game.

And for the first time, I really learned how to let God love on me.

((((( )))))

If you are struggling with a life that isn't working for you, perhaps this isn't the time for giving up but for soldiering on. It's time to dig in your heels, put some skin in the game, and fight the beast of depression. Then you can let God give you your victory.

Depression had me seized up like the Apple rainbow death wheel, but the God of hope brought me back to life. And He can do the same for you.

((((( )))))

I'm not going to tell you it will be easy or that healing will happen in a miraculous moment, but it can happen for you. My journey out of depression was a process. In this book I will open up my arsenal to arm you with some of the weapons I took on that journey. They helped me in my battle against the dark lord of depression. Your own journey will, of course, be different than mine. But one similarity is that it will probably start with understanding God differently, and therefore understanding your own life differently.

Your own path out of depression will not be pain-free. Mine wasn't. But I decided to stop crying and start sweating. Fact is, I have found some of my best inspiration in those who become elite military men and women—the Rangers, the Navy SEALs, the Delta Force, the Green Berets, and all the others who go through a rigorous process to become overcomers.

These elite fighters go through unimaginable pain to learn how to become stronger and more focused. One of the secrets of the SEALs is what they call "cognitive restructuring," which boils down to this: You say something is good even when it is terrible in order to adjust your mind to going through difficult experiences. No matter what horrible things happen to you as a SEAL, you just flash a wicked little smile and say, "Good times." That includes experiencing 96 hours of sleep deprivation, getting hypothermia during conditioning in frigid seas, and dodging bullets while you are being shot at. It's a process of convincing your brain that it can find pleasure even in the most extreme struggles.

Was this what the prophet Joel was thinking about when he said, "Let the weak say, I am strong"? (Joel 3:10 KJV).

Speaking a message of hope, regardless of what you are facing at this moment, will help train your brain to think differently. Because, in reality, this present moment is only *this* moment. It isn't forever. And you can count on the God of hope to write a better ending than what you are experiencing in the middle of your story.

The God who is a healer is always closer than you might recognize in the moment of darkness. He is the Light.

As Jacob realized, "Surely the LORD is in this place; and I knew it not" (Genesis 28:16 KJV).

In my darkest days, even when I wasn't aware of His presence, God was as near to me as my very breath.

((((( )))))

Jesus had only three years to change the world, and He still found time to have banquets, go on picnics, and party with His friends. He was less busy and had more fun than any pastor I've ever met.

That, my friends, is what the ministry looks like to me these days.

Good times.

FACING THE DARK LORD

Suicide takes the lives of more than 44,965 Americans every year.

My friend Jarrid was one of them.

Jarrid was a bouncy, fun, and gifted speaker who was devoted to removing the stigma surrounding mental illness. We were close friends, and our shared mission was giving people hope. Jarrid's kinetic energy always left me in stitches. He was hilarious. I was on the phone with his family just a few hours before he lost his personal battle with depression, totally oblivious to how dark his despair had grown.

How could this have happened?

Trying to find answers shortly after his death, I grieved right along with the author of Lamentations. As the poet watched Jerusalem get sacked by her enemies, he wrote a book centered around mourning. The word "lamentation" literally means "how?" Have you ever faced a tragedy, trauma, trial, or tribulation, and asked yourself, "*How* could this have happened?" Well, that's what Lamentations is asking.

Once a year, Jewish congregations read the book aloud, and everyone comes to acknowledge and grieve everything they have lost over the past year. Instead of burying their grief with comforting memes, they give it full expression. After all, the demon cannot be driven out until it is named.

The Bible teaches us not to sweep grief under the rug but to expose it, face it, sit with it, and ask ourselves, "How?" That's a crucial part of the grieving process.

(((( ))))

A week and a half after the last time I'd hung out with Jarrid, I learned that he had taken his own life. My heart was broken for him and for the family he left behind. It still hurts.

His death has only made me more determined to help others who might be facing a similar temptation. To help them see that a better life is ahead, and that no matter how tough things might be right now, they should never give up. They should remember that God wants to wrap His loving arms around them and carry them through the crisis.

(((( ))))

So many people struggle every day with finding a reason to go on with their lives, battling the pain and emptiness and hopelessness depression leaves in its wake. And the alarming number of suicides, especially among the young, are evidence that we are in a battle of life and death... literally. So many young people are flirting with darkness.

Everybody has a bad day now and then. Or even a bad week or two. I guess that's just part of living in a world where some awfully bad things happen. But that's not primarily what I am talking about in this book. I am talking about what you can do to combat the kind of ongoing depression that saps the joy out of life, leaving you feeling tired and sad and aimless and hopeless and helpless. The kind that makes you question whether life is really worth living. The kind that awakens with you in the morning and stalks you all through the day.

I know what that is like because I have been there.

My story is about how I learned to slay that fearsome dark lord of depression.

He has worsted me many a time. I have lost many a skirmish. But I have learned to stare him down. I have taken up arms against him. I stood my ground and found the strength I needed. I quenched the power of his flame. It's been an epic quest, worthy of Homer, and you can join me in being the hero of your own story about defeating that dark lord.

I have walked away from that battle with traumas and scars, but with wounds I can now turn into wisdom. I have a new sense of hope, a new source of strength, and a new confidence in the power of God's love to rescue me from the darkness.

The victory wasn't easy. It didn't take place in a moment's time, and it took some smart steps on my part. It required some changes in the way I thought about life and the way I lived it. Frankly, like all heroic battles, I've had to break a sweat. But I've emerged from my own skirmishes with depression with the conviction that we don't have to learn to live with it. It can be defeated. There may be many battles—some of them bloody and barbaric—but you can win the war.

You don't have to give in, or give up, or wish that someday you might get better. You can do something about the way you feel. And you can help your friends who might be in the middle of such a battle to find their way to peace and freedom.

I know Jarrid would be pleased to see me help others in the very battle that brought him down. And I imagine he is part of the cheering section in heaven for everyone who is growing weary in the fight. For it is a battle that can be won!

We will all have to endure losses and bear crosses, but we will not accept defeat. In Joshua 1:3, God promised Joshua that wherever the sole of his foot touched, that soil belonged to him. Then he draws up the outlines of the promised land. It belonged to the Israelites, with one caveat: They had to march through the breadth and length of the land. They had to measure it off with their own feet. Guess what? They never did that to more than one-third of the property! Thus, they never possessed more than one-third.[1] God told them to possess their possessions, but two-thirds eluded their dominion. Why settle for one-third of God's promises when there's so much milk and honey left untapped? There will be skirmishes in the promised land and blood in the battle, but total victory can be ours if we are willing to go on the adventure.

When the Marquis of Salisbury was criticized for his Colonial policies, he simply replied: "Gentlemen, get larger maps."[2]

Let's expand our horizons, explore our potential, and set foot on the sum total of the soil of Canaan. We will fight depression until we lay claim to every promise of hope that God offers us. I for one won't settle for one-third. I'm measuring off all the promised land. Care to join me?

YOU'RE IN
GOOD COMPANY

Some people seem to think that those who struggle with depression are weak. I don't accept that idea. In fact, those who face down depression and work through it are some of the strongest of all.

Maybe depression needs a new press agent or PR guy. Could it be that depression has gotten a bad rap? Maybe the struggle with depression is a sign that something powerful inside you needs to be rechanneled in a better direction. Maybe depression can be sublimated into a focused energy and a powerful force in your life.

If you are struggling, you are in good company.

Leo Tolstoy wrote *Anna Karenina* while in the throes of depression. At the moment in his life when he was questioning its very meaning, he was writing one of the masterpieces of Russian literature.

Buzz Aldrin was a legendary astronaut, a man who walked on the moon and accomplished a five-and-a-half-hour spacewalk. Back on Earth, he started suffering from depression and alcoholism (what do you do next if you have trod on the very surface of the moon?). He didn't give in to his emotions but instead served as chairman of the National Mental Health Association to help others.

Calvin Coolidge, American's thirtieth president, struggled with depression after the death of his son. But he still led the nation for his term of office.

Marlon Brando, arguably the greatest actor of his generation, experienced chronic depression throughout his life. Yet he turned in performances that are still among the best in the history of cinema.

Terry Bradshaw was a Hall of Fame quarterback for the Pittsburg Steelers. He was diagnosed with clinical depression and found it necessary to take antidepressants, but after a successful football career he went on to become a popular on-air commentator.

Jim Carrey, famous for his manic humor, has openly discussed his history of depression. He turned his personal pain into jokes that made us all laugh.

Winston Churchill had a name for his depression. He called it the "black dog." His diagnosis was bipolar disorder, but this didn't keep him from leading the charge to save Western civilization during World War II and later winning a Nobel Prize for literature.

Carrie Fisher, beloved as Princess Leia in the *Star Wars* films, was bipolar and dealt with manic depressive disorder.

Ernest Hemingway was one of countless great writers who struggled with deep depression.

So did Janet Jackson, Kurt Cobain, and Olympian Greg Louganis.

After her marriage broke apart, J.K. Rowling found a way to deal with her depression by writing the magical adventures of Harry Potter.

So, if you struggle with dark thoughts sometimes, take some comfort that you are in good company. You might be a wizard in a world of muggles.

((((( )))))

Each of the people mentioned above were attacked by serious bouts of depression. And each of them was able to turn that depression into fuel for their creativity.

That gives me hope.

And it reminds me that I am not alone in the struggle.

Nor are you in yours.

((((( )))))

Think about the difference between two of our American presidents. Abraham Lincoln's first serious bout of depression occurred when he was in his twenties, and he wrestled with it the rest of his life. He lost his son, had a difficult marriage, and struggled with his emotional stability during the Civil War. Franklin Pierce was our fourteenth president. His life was swallowed by tragedies, both personal and professional. None of his sons survived into adulthood. After the death of his eleven-year-old son in a train accident, both he and his wife were left with the wreckage of their lives, and he had to shoulder all the responsibilities of being the leader of the nation. His wife slowly went mad, and Pierce took to the bottle, drinking himself to an early death. Sometimes he was so drunk during cabinet meetings that he struggled to pay attention. Historians rank him as one of the least effective and least memorable presidents.

How do you deal with adversity? Consider the contrast of these two American leaders. Lincoln chose to work through his depression and became one of our greatest presidents. Pierce became an alcoholic and has largely been forgotten.

How will you respond to your problems?

PART TWO

DEFEATING

DEPRESSION

THERE WILL BE
BLOOD IN THE BATTLE

Martin Paulus, who is the director and president of the Laureate Institute for Brain Research, discovered that resilient brains respond to emotion differently. In his experiments with the Navy SEALs, he found that their brains could respond more quickly than the normal population when a color clue signaled they were about to see an emotional picture. They anticipated more quickly than average and were able to nimbly jump between different types of emotions. Because letting go of emotions is difficult for most people, who get stuck in emotional processes, they cannot adjust their emotions on the fly. But because of the training the SEALs receive, they are more resilient, and their brains grow stronger through their experiences, just as our muscles grow stronger by working them.[1]

We can, like the SEALs, learn how to control and deal with our emotions, and I'll be sharing in this book many of the things that have helped me to do that.

((((( )))))

In the next several chapters I would like to unglue you from your traumatic emotional experiences, reframe your pain, and retrain your brain to become mentally resilient. I'm going to give you the warrior weapons you need to fight the dastardly dark lord of depression. I'll share with you some of the things that have helped me to defeat my depression and keep it away. All of these, in various ways, have contributed to climbing out of my own personal pit.

I'm calling them weapons because I believe we are in a war; our journey isn't on a cruise ship but a battleship. We are doing battle with dark thoughts and dark emotions and dark perspectives in our heart and in our mind. They are ultimately rooted in our warfare against the psychospiritual forces of evil that play on the battlefield of our biochemistry. Like any weapon, though, you aren't helped just by knowing it's available. You must take the weapon in hand and wield it. Only then can your depression be defeated.

Just as SEALs unglue themselves from their emotions, we must soldier on, embark on a brand-new journey—a journey of hope—and fight for what we don't feel. In "It Only Takes 5 Seconds to Change Your life," Mel Robbins wrote, "According to neuroscientist Antonio Damasio, it's our feelings that decide for us 95 percent of the time." But as children of God, we have the power to choose to "count it all joy" and move on from the emotions that leave us stuck in the past.

The main thing, before anything else, is that you must show up for the battle and be brave. Your suffering has as much meaning as the courage with which you choose to meet it. There will be blood in the battle, and we won't escape completely unscathed, but victory is ours. Paul said the weapons of our warfare are "mighty through God to the pulling down of strong holds" (2 Corinthians 10:4 KJV).

So, I thought I would share some of the ones that have worked for me. I'll open the arsenal so that you're armed to the teeth and ready to win.

Into the breaches once more, my friends!

WEAPON #1:
PRAYER WALKS

When it comes to defeating depression, the most important thing you can do is to look to the Strong One for strength. You don't have to go it alone. You shouldn't. If you want to get your head and heart in the right space, you need to start with prayer.

Scientists have discovered three things that have a significant impact on brain health. Each of them is beneficial to thinking properly and dealing with reality in a healthy way. Each of them is also helpful for someone struggling with depression.

The first is exercise, which gets the blood flowing through your system and gets oxygen streaming to your brain. Sometimes a good run, lifting weights, or shooting hoops will clear out the cobwebs and help you feel better and have a healthier mindset about your problems. Researchers tell us that jogging for 40 minutes has the same effect as taking an antidepressant.[1] This kind of exercise creates an amazing runner's high as it releases endorphins. It invites happier thoughts!

The second is reading, which gives your brain the workout *it* needs. Reading is like aerobics for the mind. Plus, reading will make you smarter and enrich your life. Guaranteed. It'll help you see things more clearly, including your own life. And you never have to worry about tearing your Achilles tendon by reading a book. There are no adverse side effects. Reading just improves your brain. #duh.

Those seem like no-brainers. Pun intended. The third thing that will improve your brain health is...wait for it...

Prayer.

Scientists have discovered that when people are intentional and focused in their prayers, the frontal lobe of the brain is stimulated, firing up the neurons to perform at peak intellectual capacity.[2] In other words, a life-style based around talking with God is great for your brain. And when your brain is working as it should, it will help you deal with your emotions in a healthier way.

Praying has a demonstrable impact on your gray cells. When you pray to a loving God, a lot of activity is going on in your anterior cingu-late cortex, which is the part of the brain that makes you feel safe and secure. It results in feeling comfortable in God's presence and gives you some warm and fuzzy feelings. It also makes you more compassion-ate and empathetic. Which is why it makes sense that God tells us to pray for our enemies!

It's hard to keep someone on your hit list when they are also on your prayer list...

((((( )))))

You've probably already noticed how much I love research. But my conclusions are not just based on evidence from a science experiment. When it comes to prayer, the science only confirms what I already know to be true. As the saying goes, a man with an argument will always be at the mercy of a man with an experience. As clear as the data might be, the real reason I'm an avid believer in prayer is because

I have encountered its results time and time again in my life. I can't even begin to count the number of instances where I've started a time of prayer feeling depressed and discouraged and then emerged from it feeling joyful and centered.

Ezekiel 46:9 says that when God's people enter the presence of the Lord for solemn feasts, if they enter by the south gate they should leave by the north gate. Because when we truly encounter God, we always leave that meeting a different person than we were when we came in. I often start my prayer time feeling down (south), but I almost always finish feeling up (north).

When we turn our cares into prayers, our problems into petitions, our stresses into supplications, and our worries into worship, the Bible promises a peace that will guard our hearts (Philippians 4:7). The word for "guard" in Greek is used of a sentinel keeping watch over a prisoner. Prayer invites the peace of God to keep our thoughts in captivity so the bad ones don't run amok!

((((( )))))

God taps into souls like the FBI taps into phones. He's always listening.

And He always answers knee mail.

((((( )))))

I pray best when I get out of my chair and take a walk.

Nothing fortifies my soul, buttresses my concentration, clears my mind, or makes me feel a surge of inner peace as much as a good prayer walk. Nothing has been more helpful to me in overcoming depression than a good brisk walk—just me and God.

The Bible records the stories of those who "walked with God," and I'm pretty sure that, for many of them, actual walking was involved.

I'm not one of those people who can sit in a lotus position, close my eyes, and empty my mind. I just can't manage it. I'm not even that good at sitting quietly with folded hands and a bowed head. (Which, by the way, the Bible *never* suggests as the ultimate model for prayer.) Instead, I like to walk while I talk!

There's just something about walking.

Adam walked with God in the cool of the day. Enoch walked with God and was translated into His presence. Paul told his fellow believers that they should walk worthy of the calling they have received. God invited Abraham to "walk before me" (Genesis 17:1).

I especially love long walks on the beach. I know that sounds like something from an online dating profile, but it's true. When I can take a trek along the ocean shore and literally talk out loud with God, I am more fulfilled than at almost any other time. We chat about my dreams and desires, and He gives me such a superabundance of hope that I leave my one-on-one with Him having loads of encouragement to share with others.

Sometimes my prayer walks are in the city at night, under the stars and streetlights—just me and God. Walking is good for the brain. It helps enlarge the hippocampus, which is the seat of memory.[3] So, when your trouble doubles, go on a prayer walk and get double for your trouble!

My prayer walks fill me full so that I have something to give to others. At the same time, they soothe my spirit, remove the smog from my noggin, and put pep in my step.

(((( ))))

I've heard people suggest there is something self-centered about praying for yourself. This isn't remotely true. There is nothing selfish about praying for your own needs. Frankly, this should probably be priority one for your time of prayer. Have you ever noticed that in the Psalms, the prayer book of the Bible, nearly all the psalms contain an expression of passionate concern for the situation in which the writer finds himself? Also, nearly half of them contain laments—statements of hurt and complaint and general expressions of unhappiness. These are a big part of what happens when we pray candidly.

Be honest. Raw. Real. Talk to Him like you would talk to your most trusted friend, and don't worry about a lot of pious posturing or trying to say the correct thing. Jesus told His disciples that He no longer called them servants but friends (John 15:15). Like Abraham and Moses, you're invited to talk face-to-face, just the way you would open up to your bestie.

I'm not embarrassed to say it. I love that I'm chill with the Almighty.

((((( )))))

The kind of prayer that helps defeat depression is the kind of prayer that pulls no punches.

I can even gossip to God like a middle school girl. Seriously. There are things I have to get off my chest lest they crush me. That's what one of the psalmists did. He told God all about his traitorous friends and even asked God to break the teeth of his enemies. There were no holds barred.

He's a God of love, but He completely understands when love isn't our first emotion. Frankly, He's not shocked or surprised by some of our darker thoughts or juicy tidbits. It's not as though He mutters under His breath, "Really? I can't believe she said that! I had no idea!"

He already knows our dark places and our dark thoughts. He's aware of our frustrations and complaints and when we think life isn't fair. The psalmists poured out their complaints before God. We can do the same.

Sometimes we just need to get all the angst out of our system and into the open. It's so much more constructive to have these angry conversations with God than to bottle up our emotions because it doesn't seem appropriate to express them. He can handle all of them.

When we are willing to be honest, we receive His love and grace. When we complain to others, though, the best we can hope for is a little pity. So, take it to Him. We can either complain to people and get their pity or complain to the Prince of Peace and get His power.

As Joyce Meyer puts it, "I don't have to complain and remain."

I can "praise and be raised."[4]

((((( )))))

The way you think about God affects the way your brain processes your emotions.

Scientists have devised methods of using cat-scans and MRIs to observe brain activity during meditation and prayer. Here is what they found:

Praying to a God whom you perceive to be loving and merciful and kind helps you develop richer, thicker gray matter in your prefrontal cortex, the portion of your cranial package that is responsible for focus, concentration, and creative thinking.[5] Maybe the psalmist was onto something when he said, "Early will I seek thee" (Psalm 63:1 KJV) because the prefrontal cortex is most active immediately after you wake up. That's why it is best to do your creative work in the morning—even if you feel groggy at first.

On the other hand, when you pray to a God you perceive to be angry and judgmental, just looking for an excuse to smite you for your misdeeds, your amygdala lights up, which is the place where the emotions of fear, anger, and stress are located. You'll experience these unpleasant and unhealthy reactions: a rise in blood pressure, more tension and anxiety, and a harder time overlooking the mistakes of others. You'll also have a harder time forgiving others. This is how we respond when we are trying to placate a God whom we see as vengeful.

So, doesn't it make more sense to cast your cares on the God who cares for you so that your amygdala will lose its grip on your feelings? Stress and fear and anger will retreat. You'll have a crisper focus and deepen your ability to think creatively. You might even experience the warm fuzzies and find it easier to relate well with other people.

When you perceive God as being a wrathful, easily-ticked-off, tribal deity who is just waiting to catch you doing something wrong, it's hard to have a healthy emotional life.

When you see God as loving and caring, it's much easier to deal with your feelings and emotions.

That, my friends, is neurotheology in a nutshell.

((((( ))))))

Martin Luther wrote, "Prayer is not overcoming God's reluctance but instead laying hold of His willingness." Jesus said that if you ask your dad for bread, He won't hand you a stone; if you ask for a fish, He won't give you a serpent, and if you ask for an egg, He won't put a scorpion in your hand (Matthew 7:9-10; Luke 11:11-12). This was actually a clever statement. In the ancient Near East, limestones looked like loaves of bread, so a dad could trick his child and cause some broken teeth. And the word "serpent" can be translated as an eel, which was one of the forbidden food groups in Levitical law (seafood was more than fish in those times!). Plus, there is a pale variety of scorpion that curls up in a ball when it is at rest, and it looks kind of like an egg.

Jesus's point is that God doesn't want to trick you. He wants to bless you. Notice the progression: bread is a pretty bland item, but it takes care of your daily needs; a fish is a tasty treat, but eggs are the best of all! It wasn't until the New Testament times that people began to raise chickens, and they were still an uncommon luxury.[6] So, don't limit Providence to bread, or even fish, but reach for the eggs! Heaven is more ready to give than you are to ask.

WEAPON #2: SCRIPTURE SCHOLAR SCUBA GEAR

What do you usually hear when people start to talk about the Bible? It's normally something like "God has a plan for your life!" Now, that's pretty good news, though it is also pretty generic. And when you are in a battle against depression, it might not sound very helpful. The truth is that God really *does* have a plan for your life, but it's a lot more magical and a lot more complicated than that nifty little phrase can contain. Your life and its meaning are not linear. The universe isn't composed of nice, neat right angles.

There is infinite complexity in the world. Just ponder the fractal geometry of clouds and shorelines and snowflakes. The closer you look at them, the greater number of shapes you'll see. Zooming in for a closer look at almost anything reveals details you can't see with the naked eye. The closer you look, the more complex it becomes. Infinitely, so it seems.

And then there's Einsteinian relativity, astrophysical anomalies, and quantum theory.

This world can seem like one puzzling place.

So why do we often expect the answers to our questions to be simple ones?

((((( )))))

Just as the world is complex, so is the Bible. It's ingenious, intricate, and involved. It's layered with meaning and metaphor. And it's a communication from God. Hello? Why would we ever expect it to be simple?

Sure, you can skim the surface of the Bible, looking for a few little inspiring memes. Similarly, you can jet ski over the surface of the water, which may be a lot of fun, but it doesn't tell you much about what's down there in the fathomless deeps—a world teeming with life and mystery.

Here's an important question: Do you want to dog-paddle on the surface of the Bible or plunge into its depths? Let's be like SEALs and strap on our oxygen tanks. No more playing in the shallows. Let's see how far down this thing can go.

If you are willing to take the deep dive, you'll discover it has answers that can help you emerge from the darkness of depression.

I'd like you to join me as I don my Scripture scholar scuba gear and descend into some deep places, leaving the shallows behind as we explore ten themes of God's big plan for our lives.

Take a deep breath.

Here we go...

((((( )))))

Number one: God wants to effectuate the universe. This is just a fancy way of saying He is the Creator. He doesn't just have a plan for your life—He has a plan for the entire universe. When the Bible says, "In the beginning God created the heavens and the earth" (Genesis 1:1), the Hebrew verb for "create" is a word that is never used for human creativity, but only for that which originates from God. Journalist Franklin P. Jones wrote, "Originality is the art of concealing your sources," and all human creators are just archaeologists. God alone is capable of pure invention. The message of the first chapter of the Bible is that God created *ex nihilo* (out of nothing). He didn't refashion existing stuff but instead caused something to exist that had not previously existed.

Let me introduce you to the trinity of trinities.[1] In the first verse of Genesis we see God creating the great scientific trinity of time (in the beginning), space (the heavens), and matter (the earth), which are the primary building blocks of our universe.

And each of these building blocks has three properties or principles within it. Time consists of past, present, and future. Space consists of height, width, and depth. And matter consists of solid, liquid, and gas. Voilà! The trinity of trinities. God is the ultimate scientist, and He is an artist working on a very big canvas. He knows what He is doing.

So keep in mind that you and your problems are not the center of everything. You fit into a much bigger scheme. Apocalyptic scientists foresee the earth being swallowed up by the sun in five billion years, but God assures us the universe is unfolding as it should.

((((( )))))

Number two: God wants to engender a new humanity. As Paul explains, God's purpose was to create in Himself one new humanity (Ephesians 2:15). This is at the root of everything. In the story of the Garden of Eden, the snake lied to Adam and Eve, saying, "If you eat the forbidden fruit, you will be like God" (Genesis 3). But two chapters earlier we are told that Adam (the Hebrew word for "the human") was made in God's likeness. In other words, humans are already like God! But the enemy wanted to imply that God was holding out on Adam, that he was missing out on something important. He was tantalizing Adam with a false narrative.

Of course, the enemy is still busy doing the same thing to you and me today. He wants to make us believe that God isn't giving us the best when in fact He has already reached down to offer it to us. We are, the Genesis story tells us, image bearers for the Divine, mirroring God's creative attributes to the world. That is our identity. No matter how messed up humanity becomes, no matter how often we might lose the plot, God is redeeming His creation. He wants to make us new—a new kind of humanity. We are, Scripture tells us, "a new creation" (2 Corinthians 5:17), which in Greek literally means "a new species." We are updated from being Homo sapiens to being Hope-o-sapiens. No matter how genocidal, tragic, and wasteful humans might be, there is no reason to despair over our race. God has imbedded His very likeness into our DNA, and all creation awaits the revealing of the sons and daughters of God!

If we understand a greater narrative is unfolding, of which we are a part, then we can embrace where God is taking us. We have an incredible, mind-bending destiny just around the corner.

((((( )))))

Number three: God wants to eradicate our fear. Fear does so much damage to our lives. When we are afraid, physical and chemical reactions occur within us, and many different hormones and neurotransmitters are activated. All that activity takes a toll on us, body and soul.

But the good news is that we can be free from fear. The most oft-repeated command in the Bible is "do not fear." It's in the Book at least 200 times. The Bible tells us that we have not been given a spirit of fear but of *love* (2 Timothy 1:7). And perfect love drives out fear (1 John 4:18). My body is a temple for this spirit—a spirit of love and not fear—and therefore I am incapable of fear. I. Cannot. Fear.

Did you get that?

When we are afraid, we are living in an imaginary reality because fear comes from believing a lie.

What is fear? Zig Ziglar used this acronym: False Evidence Appearing Real!

When we are afraid, it's only because we aren't seeing the big picture.

So, we do not need to trust anxiety's whispers but can embrace a bold attitude toward life.

Ziglar also shared a better response to fear: Face Everything And Rise! Now that's an acronym I can get on board with!

((((( )))))

Number four: The Bible reveals God's plan to encourage our love. Jesus said that all the law and prophets hang on love (Matthew 22:34-40). We were never made to be alone. We were made for love. We are a social species. Did you know that grief is largely a form of separation anxiety?[2] Look at how many animals run in packs. Think about what happens when you leave the house and your dog starts to panic. He won't be comforted until you return. He needs you.

Similarly, we need one another. God created us for community, which is why Jesus said, "Where two or three gather in my name, there am I with them" (Matthew 18:20). Jesus is the image of the Father, and God is love (1 John 4:8), but in order to show love, you need a neighbor. We were not meant just to experience God by ourselves but with each other. We were made for love.

So, we must not try to live out our lives on our own. We need the love and companionship of others.

((((( )))))

Number five: God wants to empower resurrection realities to burst through the cracks here and now! Every time Jesus predicted His crucifixion, He also predicted His resurrection. The message of God's power at work in our lives in not just about our eternal destiny. His purpose isn't just to get you into heaven tomorrow. His resurrection power is for today and tomorrow and the day after that.

The big message of the New Testament is that Jesus has defeated all the power of death and darkness and evil. He was crucified and died and was buried. But He didn't stay in the tomb. He got up and walked out. The tomb is empty.

So, we can embrace the resurrection power of Jesus for our own lives. We have a spiritual power within us that can put darkness to flight.

We don't have to stay in the tomb of our own troubles. We can walk right out the door because the same power that raised Jesus from the dead animates us.

Do you want the good news first or the good news first? Gospel indeed.

((((( )))))

Number six: God wants to enlighten the eyes of our understanding (Ephesians 1:18). One of Jesus's miracles was to open the eyes of a blind man and give him back his sight. This is something Jesus still wants to do for us today—give us back a clear vision of life.

Before Jesus was arrested, He did only *two* miracles in Jerusalem: healing the lame at the pool of Bethesda and the blind at the pool of Siloam. Why these two miracles, specifically? Because when David founded the city of Jerusalem, the inhabitants taunted, "Even the lame and blind could ward you off" (2 Samuel 5:6). Nevertheless, David conquered it. The lame and the blind could not overcome David's military, nor the Son of David's healing ministry. Jesus opened the eyes of the blind. Indeed, the Bible says He will give a new perspective for those who have eyes to see.

So, we can be thankful that God wants to give us new eyes to see our lives and struggles. The same God who enlightens our eyes also is the One who can bring healing to our lives—and He does it on His own schedule.

(((( ))))

Number seven: God wants to ennoble our work. Some have suggested that the Bible is the first book in ancient literature to put a high premium on blue-collar work. We tend to think of Jesus as a carpenter, just like his father, Joseph. But in reality, a carpenter was more like a general contractor, and working with stone would also be part of the profession. Joseph likely worked as a stonemason in Sepphoris, an urban area about four miles from Nazareth. And because the father would usually teach his profession to his son, it isn't a stretch to think of Jesus as a construction worker! God loves work. It isn't just something we have to do because of the curse. Adam had a job as a gardener before the fall.

So, whatever you put your hand to—whether you work in a biscuit factory or a corporate office—do it to the glory of God.

Sometimes doing some good old-fashioned manual labor can be one of the best cures for depression.

(((( ))))

Number eight: God wants to edit our narrative. The Bible is filled with stories, and when read as a whole, it offers one big, profound narrative—the story of God reclaiming splintered humanity…and not only restoring it, but actually taking it to a new level.

The Author of your faith (Hebrews 12:2 kjv) has all your days written in His book (Psalm 139:16). Whatever your current circumstances, you can be assured that He has not lost the plot. He is about to turn the page on your pains. He will turn those pains into pangs as you give birth to your destiny.

So, we need to be ready to allow God to rewrite our stories. To give them new and unexpected meanings. To add in positive twists and turns we never saw coming. If you are in the middle of what seems to be a tragedy, you can let the Master rewrite the meaning of your life. He is the One who can turn every story into a story of hope.

((((( )))))

Number nine: God wants to eternalize Eden. The garden is not just where humanity came from; it's also where it's going. A river and a tree of life are in Genesis just as they are in Revelation's garden city. In Eden, Adam exercised his dominion in naming the animals, and in ancient Jewish culture, to name something was a recognition of ownership. Just as the first Adam gave names to the animals, so the Last Adam promises to give us a stone with our new name on it, one that only the one who receives it knows (Revelation 2:17). Scientists have discovered that dolphins choose their own names at birth,[3] and so we will have a new identity when we are given our true name in eternity.

((((( )))))

Number ten: God wants to elect us to kingship. He wants to do for you what Aslan did for the children of Narnia. He wants to crown you kings and queens under His sovereign rule.

Jesus lived a pretty normal life until He turned 30, and then He was baptized and began His public ministry. It was at that time that He did His first miracle. Thirty was the age when a person in Jewish culture came into his father's inheritance. That's why Jesus was baptized at 30! He has that same kind of heritage awaiting you and me. Perhaps you have already stepped into it. If not, embrace your royalty today. It is your high and holy destiny.

Jesus promised His disciples that they would do even greater things than He had done (John 14:12), which is amazing when you think about His miracles, His healings, and His teachings. Scholars don't agree on what that means, but what all scholars do agree on is that Jesus did not say we would do *lesser* things than He has done. Christ assures us that greatness is our lot. Toward the end of His earthly life, He said, "Do not be afraid, little flock, for your Father has been pleased to give you the kingdom (Luke 12:32). Jesus didn't just come to Earth to teach us how to live or lead us to personal salvation. He came to inaugurate a new Kingdom, the Kingdom of God. And that Kingdom is composed of His sons and daughters, His own chosen kings and queens.

So, remember that when life isn't going well right now, you have a destiny that is beyond tomorrow. You have been chosen to be one of God's royalty, to reign with Him in His new Kingdom. That truth certainly provides us a great light for our present darkness. We can step into the role He has chosen for us. We are destined for greatness as high kings and queens of Narnia. Further up and further in, following in the pawprints of the Lion of the tribe of Judah.

(((( )))))

When you are flying in a plane at 30,000 feet, you'll see things you just can't see when you are on the ground. It's the same with the Bible. You can get lost in all the individual teachings and laws and stories and fail to see the bigger picture. Getting this bigger picture changes the way you read the Bible and changes the way you look at yourself and your world.

A grand, heroic epic is being written, and you are one of the chosen characters. How will you respond to your exalted role? Will you let your emotions, your past history, or your present struggles keep you from joyfully fulfilling your part in God's Kingdom plan? Or will you join me in embracing it, casting aside everything that gets in the way of living with hope?

If you feel as if you are going through hell, try going through the Bible. It's one heaven of a book!

9

WEAPON #3: THE MAGIC NUMBER OF GREATNESS

I got to a point in my struggle with depression where something needed to change. I was suffering so badly I finally decided to do something about it.

There are two kinds of pain: 1) the pain that hurts you and 2) the pain that changes you.

I decided to stop licking my wounds and go to war. Anything was better than being trapped like a prisoner in my own skull, alone with my thoughts and unable to turn off the terrors in my brain.

In *The Problem of Pain,* C.S. Lewis remarks on the difference between the suffering of animals and the suffering of humans. The former, he said, merely have sentience, but the latter have consciousness. It's one thing to bear pain automatically or subconsciously, but Lewis argued that the problem of human pain is that we are so acutely aware of it. When a man's tooth aches, it's not only the toothache itself, but the experience of lying there thinking about the toothache that makes it that much worse.

I've always had an overactive brain. My friends tell me it's my greatest strength…and my greatest weakness. Just last night my friend Bo joked that while I know a lot about the anomalous composition of matter in the universe, I didn't know how to properly eat a burrito. I still tear it apart with my fingers like a little kid. And for this I get sorely, and deservedly, trolled by my friends. Yeah, I'm the guy who studies quantum mechanics and astrophysics, but I still can't seem to figure out how to work my washing machine.

I just can't find the switch to shut off my overactive brain. I get trapped inside an endless hamster wheel of thought and frequently suffer a Kierkegaardian existential nausea.

So, I had to get out of my head to start getting better.

I needed something to distract me—a worthy goal that could help me escape the angst. A purpose.

The 10,000-hour rule saved my life.

(((( ))))

I touched on this in chapter 3. In his book *Outliers*, Malcolm Gladwell demonstrated that to be truly great at anything, you have to put in 10,000 hours of practice. People such as world chess champion Bobby Fischer, businessman Bill Joy, and IBM founder Bill Gates are among the many examples Gladwell gives of people who excelled because they accelerated. They focused and worked hard and gave at least 10,000 hours to becoming the best at what they did. Gladwell showed that whether you want to be a fiction writer or a master criminal, a hockey player or a pianist, 10,000 hours was the magic number of greatness. I bent my mind to that goal as a writer and speaker.[1]

I resolved to stop wasting my energies processing psychological trauma and to go in a diametrically opposed direction. Instead of despairing over why my dreams weren't coming to pass, I decided to commit myself to working my fingers to the bone to ensure they did.

Psychologist John Hayes "looked at how long it took the best compos-ers of all time to create their first great work. He found that nobody, including Mozart [who was a child prodigy], had produced a piece of work of any significance until about 10 years after they had first taken up music...No amount of innate talent, even in a field of 'genius' such as music, could overcome the years of practice necessary to create work. Someone may be talented, they may be lucky, but they still have to go through 10 years of practice in order to become a master."[2]

When Churchill came to power during World War II, he said this as he was being inaugurated into office as prime minister: "I offer you noth-ing save blood, toil, tears and sweat." Like Churchill, I was ready to go to battle. I knew the path would be difficult, but I was ready to claim my own finest hour.

Getting better starts with just getting off your tush and doing something.

So, I did.

My goal was to become a writer and a speaker, so I put in the needed hours. I nearly worked myself to death, but it was infinitely better than brooding. I found the effort cathartic and fulfilling. My spirits began to lift.

I figured I had two options: 1) Either get discouraged that my dreams were not coming to pass or 2) spend the effort of getting prepared for when they did.

Legendary preacher Charles Spurgeon advised his students to stop worrying about when they would get their shot at speaking and con-centrate instead on their ability, and then let God take care of the opportunity. In other words, quit fretting over the *how* and focus on the *what*. I took these words to heart and focused on my skill set as I improved my craft. Our English word "amateur" comes from a French, Italian, and Latin root which means "to love." A novice works when he loves the process and it feels good. A professional is someone who works seven days a week whether he feels like it or not.

Today my TV show, *Hope Generation*, is on 20 different networks in more than 180 countries, and my radio show is heard on more than 400 stations daily. I get to speak in stadiums and arenas. My "overnight success" came through hours of hard work. Let's face it. If you knew me, you wouldn't think any of this was at all likely.

(((( )))))

How you'll spend your 10,000 hours may be different from how I spent mine, but you'll find, as I did, a clearer focus and a way of getting off the existential treadmill of despair. It'll transform your life. By the age of 21, the average American has put 10,000 hours of practice into computer and video games.[3] Why not use those hours for something more productive?

How hard you hustle in the darkness determines how brightly you shine in the spotlight. To prepare for speaking to people, I got really good at lecturing my furniture. My chairs were my captive audience. I remember that Billy Graham once said he got his start by preaching to alligators before he preached in stadiums. You have to start with the small stuff and work your way up. So, I took every opportunity that presented itself. I spoke to classes of little kids, at homeless shelters, at old folks homes, and to student clubs. I volunteered to take the opportunities others turned down. I got lots of practice. When other speakers turned an organization or a church down, I said yes...and I did this for several years.

Only the small-minded person will refuse the small task. For me, if I had an audience of four people, that was enough to get some more practice. To put in some more hours toward my 10,000-hour goal.

Jesus said that if you are faithful in a few small things, you will be given responsibility over bigger ones (Matthew 25). That sounded good to me.

((((( ))))))

Yes, sometimes I did feel like Sisyphus, the tragic hero of Greek mythology, who had to roll a boulder up a hill only to see it roll back down, then roll it back up again only for it to roll back down again. Repeatedly. I was stubborn in my pursuit. Yet it was a great weapon against despair to keep working in spite of how I felt.

Which puts me in mind of a scene from Tolkien's *The Lord of the Rings*. In the first book of that trilogy, *The Fellowship of the Ring*, a band of warriors is commissioned to travel to the ends of the earth to destroy the evil Ring of Power by casting it into Mount Doom. During their long journey, Gandalf, who was their leader, was thought to be killed in the mines of Moria. In response, Aragorn stepped up to lead the band in his stead. Amid his grief and despair, he cried out, "Farewell, Gandalf! What hope have we without you?"

Then he turned to the fellowship and said, "We must do without hope. Let us gird ourselves and weep no more. Come, we have a long road."

Like that epic trek to Mount Doom, healing is usually a long journey. We normally don't start feeling better overnight. Sometimes we must go on when we feel absolutely no hope. Our quest leads down a winding path, and it's sometimes fraught with trolls and goblins and all manner of dark creatures. But psychological heroism is possible, and such a journey is worth taking.

Like Aragorn and Frodo, I set my foot upon my own path out of depression. I gave up my flirtation with darkness and began to tread the road toward a grand purpose.

And it worked. After many, many years, the dreams I had begun to despair of finally came true. New ones came into sight. But it all began by putting one foot in front of the other.

"Hard work brings prosperity; playing around brings poverty" (Proverbs

28:19 TLB), and "Work hard and become a leader; be lazy and become a slave" (Proverbs 12:24 NLT).

It's all too easy to allow yourself to become a slave to your ennui, sadness, disappointment, and depression.

If you allow yourself to just sit around in a partly catatonic state, stuffing yourself with junk food as a form of therapy and watching countless hours of television, you will probably never start feeling better. But I tell you that if you get off the couch and venture into the world to do something toward your goals, things will start to change in your heart and mind. If you pull yourself out of bed and get going on your dreams, that's how you will begin the journey to healing your broken spirit.

I'm not saying it will be easy. It wasn't for Aragorn and the Fellowship of the Ring.

I realized I had to stop waiting for opportunities to roll up. What I needed to roll up was my sleeves and chase the opportunities.

I needed to gird myself with my armor and charge the front lines—even when it looked as though failure was likely. Frankly, it was just good to be in the battle. And like the Marines, I learned to embrace the pain, push myself beyond my limits, and run toward the danger. That was what made me happy…as long as I was making progress toward my goals. Of course, Marines almost prefer being miserable; they prefer the coldest chow, the crummiest gear, and the most awful conditions. They live by the same edict as the apostle Paul: "Suffer hardship with me as a good soldier" (2 Timothy 2:3 NASB). So, rather than waiting around for ideal circumstances, I, too, chose the warrior's way and did the work. "Go hard." That became my motto.

Good times.

(((( ))))

I want to be like John Wesley, who had big goals and the work ethic to back them up. He "preached 42,000 sermons…and travelled in coach or on horseback equal to ten times the circumference of the globe."[4] When he was a spry 83 years old, he wrote in his diary: "I am a wonder to myself…I am never tired, (such is the goodness of God) with either writing, preaching, or traveling."[5]

That is exactly how I feel now, and I plan to feel like that when I am 83. The schedule I'm keeping isn't that different from the one Wesley pursued.

I'm striving to do the very best I can manage. My grandpa worked at Disneyland on the construction of the famous Pirates of the Caribbean ride. When the great Walt Disney himself, ever the perfectionist, ever the detail guy, came to inspect their work, he told them how much he loved a certain building they had created. It was perfect. But he said it would be even better if they could move it just a couple of inches. Which meant they had to tear it down and rebuild it in a new place.

That's why Walt Disney was Walt Disney. Every detail had to be just right.

((((( )))))

Why was Jerry Rice the greatest receiver in the history of the NFL? Steve Young, who played alongside him, tells how three days after the Super Bowl, he went back down to the practice facility and found it empty except for Jerry, who was out there running routes. Young thinks that this accounts for his greatness better than any other single thing.[6]

The Niners win the Super Bowl, and instead of taking a much-deserved vacation, Jerry was running routes!

Success is doing what others won't do today to have what others can't have tomorrow.

To be honest, a lot of the time I don't *feel* like working. As my friend Rich says, "If you just do what you *want* to do, it's not going to lead you to what you want. There are things you *have* to do so you can do the things you *want* to do. We too often trade what we want in the future for what we want right now!"

Orebela Gbenga said, "Commitment means staying loyal to what you said you were going to do long after the mood you said it in has left you." If you want to be a legend in your world, it means putting in the work whether you feel like it or not. Greatness doesn't happen in a day. It happens daily. So, work hard in silence. Let your success make the noise.

(((( )))))

Hard work is one of the things that pulled me out of despair.

It can do that for you.

They refer to it as "hard work" for a reason. If you're coasting, you're probably going downhill. Pain is weakness leaving the body. Sweat is your body fat crying.

As Robert Schuller puts it, "Tough times never last, but tough people do."

Roger Federer, the Swiss tennis guru, has won a record 20 Grand Slam singles titles. He once revealed the secret of his success: "In tennis, working on your weaknesses makes you maybe an overall competitive player, but you won't be dangerous. I like to work on the strength, and that's helped me throughout my career."

Get off the couch.

Get active.

Do something.

Focus on one skill, one purpose, one goal…and get *really good* at it. Put in the necessary effort and hours into an ambition that can help you make a difference in the world. Use the power that Jesus used to rise from the dead to rise from your bed. Focus on one skill, one purpose, one goal…and get really good at it.

As Steve Jobs put it, use your ambition to put a dent in the universe!

WEAPON #4:
ENDORPHINS, ANYONE?

I'm not going to belabor this point, but I think it must be said: If you stay on the couch, you won't rise out of depression.

There's something powerful about pushing your body to the limits. Remember Jesus, who spent 40 days fasting in the wilderness. When He had tested his physical endurance, and His stomach was threatening to digest itself, He had His existential "to be or not to be" moment. He turned aside from money, sex, power, and fame, and chose to be... well, Jesus.

Of course, the enemy tempted Him with bread, which provides instant gratification but no lasting satisfaction. Carbohydrates such as pasta, breads, cakes, and cookies are called comfort food because they boost a powerful brain chemical—serotonin—which affects our moods. The comfort doesn't last long, though. Within 20 minutes of eating these processed carbs, all the benefits dissipate. Jesus took the longer view of things, saying no to His shallow cravings for food and yes to His deeper desire for union with the Father.

I've found that running is my best way of getting exercise, clearing my head, and preparing to hear from God. When I push myself to the limit, something spiritually powerful happens inside me.

Not long ago I ran for 2 hours and 22 minutes on woodland trails, alongside rivers and waterfalls, and through tall, green forests. I got lost for a while, but I didn't care. I kept running. At the end of the run the heavens opened and the sky became the color of flamingo feathers. The night was on the edge of becoming, and the day seemed as though it hadn't quite run out of things to say to itself. God revealed Himself to me. Only at the end of many miles did revelation splash across the stars.

Pushing yourself physically does something spiritual to you. As the flesh dies, the spirit awakens.

((((( ))))))

Endorphins are "structurally similar to the drug morphine" and "considered natural painkillers because they activate opioid receptors in the brain that help minimize discomfort."[1]

Running might not be the answer for everyone, but getting your body moving through exercise is part of the solution for everyone. When you find a way to push your body to its limits, you release endorphins, and they make you feel better. They awaken your brain and help you climb to the next level.

I'm not saying you have to go climb Mons Olympus (the volcano on Mars that is three times taller than Everest), but I'm simply advocating that exertion will awaken your spirit to see new planes of reality.

Hey, put down that doughnut and meet me on the running trails!

WEAPON #5:
REWRITE YOUR STORY

Sometimes we struggle from the shame we carry from our past. The trajectory of our own stories can leave us feeling as though we are at a dead end. But before we are tempted to close the book on our happiness, let us remember that *our story is still being written*, and that the past does not have to determine how our story will conclude.

Here's the best news of all: Jesus is a great Rewriter of stories!

As an infant, He was taken to Egypt to escape Herod's genocide of baby boys. Later, He returned with His parents to His homeland, was baptized with water, and spent 40 days in the wilderness undergoing temptation. These things really happened, but they have a significance beyond just giving us historical information about His life.

For when Israel was an infant country, it too was taken to Egypt. Then, as Israel returned to its homeland, it did so by passing through the waters of the Red Sea and spending 40 years in the wilderness.

Did you catch that? Both Jesus and Israel are taken to Egypt as babies, pass through the waters, and then spend 40 days/years in the wilderness.

Where do we learn about these parallels? They are highlighted in the Gospel of Matthew.

Matthew was writing to a Jewish audience…the then-modern descendants of the Israelites.

Jesus is, Matthew reveals, living out the very story of the chosen people. And He is God's chosen Son, rewriting the story of redemption.

Boom.

(((( )))))

Something more is always going on in the stories of the Bible. Here is a case in point:

The Gospels (Mark 5; Luke 8) tell the story of how Jesus met a demon-possessed guy who was living in a cemetery among the tombs. When Jesus asked the man his name, he replied, "Legion." (You'll be hard pressed to find that one in a book of suggested baby names!) Jesus took mercy on this man and cast the demons out of him.

Now, if you were a Jew in the first century and hearing this story for the first time, you would find its subtext to be jaw dropping. Here's why: Rome had shamed Israel by conquering it. When that happened, the Roman Empire sent thousands of troops—called "legions"—to march through the Jewish streets. (A legion consisted of 6,000 soldiers.) The Roman Empire, which did not acknowledge the Hebrew God, occupied the land and took control of God's chosen people. The very existence of these legions was Israel's great shame, and their very presence a reminder that the Jews were a defeated foe, that the Romans were their masters.

Do you see the subtext in this story?

When Jesus cast out Legion, He was also casting out Israel's shame.

He was retelling Israel's story!

And that same God wants to retell your story.

He wants to redeem your past and give you a new hope for the future. As Jesus promises at the tail end of the last book of the Bible, "I am making everything new!" (Revelation 21:5). He doesn't say that He makes all new things, but that He makes all things new. He finds people with a sad, old story of being trapped and shamed and hopeless and helpless, and He reworks that story into a thing of beauty.

The Author of Faith is in the business of turning stories around and creating new, happier endings.

You are not stuck with your past or limited by your present. The future is still brimming with hope. All the chapters written so far are but a preparation for the grand plot twist which is coming.

Spoiler alert: Your story has a happy ending.

WEAPON #6:
OWN YOUR ODDNESS

So, am I going to seem like a knuckle-dragging Neanderthal if I throw in a few warnings about social media? Call me a caveman, but I have to say my piece: Instagram is not exactly a great promoter of mental health. Experts say that one of the reasons why we are the most depressed generation ever is because of social media.

Remember those posters about evolution that you saw in school: from monkey to man? From the goo to the zoo? They show an ape, then a prehistoric man, then an upright featherless biped. Well, it seems as though we've gone backward thanks to social media. We spend so much time with our eyes glued to our smartphones, comparing ourselves to one another on Instagram and being overly solicitous with our likes on social media, that our bodily posture is one of being hunched over to look down at our screens. We are bent over our phone like a monkey in trousers. It's not our best look. May God once again be, as the psalmist says, the lifter of our heads!

((((   ))))

The internet can be a very good thing. However, too much of a good thing can become a bad thing when we exalt it to a (lowercase) god thing. Technology is simply a tool for expanding our preexisting human capabilities. If you put too high a premium on it, it folds in on itself and collapses.

Take a microphone and a car as two examples. Humans have been able to talk for millennia, but a microphone is only a technological device that amplifies the human voice. Humans have been able to travel for thousands of years, but a car accelerates our mode of locomotion. But when we exalt technology, it actually becomes less efficient than our previous capacities. If you turn up a microphone too loud, you get feedback, and the human voice becomes harder to hear. Or, if you have too many cars on the road, you get a traffic jam, and a person can get from one place to another faster by walking than they can in their fancy Corvette.

In the same manner, the internet can expand our ability to connect with one another, but when you overdose on social media, it destroys that linkage. Social media also quantifies followers, views, and likes, so it becomes almost impossible to refrain from comparing yourself with others. Thus, the very mechanism designed to link us together can easily destroy the very connection it was supposed to enhance. Connection becomes comparison; human interaction is replaced by digital addiction.

Yes, Instagram stories can be loads of fun to look at, but they also have a dark side. Consider when we watch them: at the most boring lull in our day when we pick up our phone to view the most exciting part of someone else's day. We look at people summiting the Matterhorn or trekking Machu Picchu or throwing a rager while we are busy gorging on Twinkies. We are watching the most interesting part of their lives when we are bored. *And they are doing the same in regard to us.* No one is interested in an Instagram about how they are sitting in their recliner stuffing their face with nachos as they gorge on an old rerun of *Lost* for the thirty-seventh time. No one posts about mowing the lawn or doing the dishes. No, the Instagram stories people choose to share give the impression that their life is one big, unending party.

It's a trick and a trap. What you are watching are the highlight reels from other people's lives.

And then what happens? You start to compare your life with their lives.

Your own life seems gray.

Your own life seems lonely.

Your own life seems sad.

((((( )))))

Almost nothing can make you unhappy more quickly than comparing your life with that of others. On the outside, everybody else's life looks more interesting. Comparison is the surest thief of your joy and contentment. It robs the happiness from your heart.

Then, after comparison comes envy, which is surely one of the ugliest emotions.

Comparison is a no-win road to travel. Even if you become prettier than anyone you know, or smarter than any of your acquaintances, or have the highest number of friends on Facebook—there will still always be someone prettier, more intellectual, and more connected than you.

Even if you conquer the world, envy will still be waiting on the summit to try to destroy you.

Once, when Julius Caesar was at leisure in Spain, he was reading about the exploits of Alexander the Great. Suddenly, those around him noticed that he had burst into tears. His companions rushed to his side and asked what was the matter. Caesar, a person of almost unimaginable power and at the very height of his fame, said this in response: "Do you not think it is matter for sorrow that while Alexander, at my age, was already king of so many peoples, I have as yet achieved no brilliant success?"[1]

It's been said: Don't be jealous of Napoleon, because Napoleon was jealous of Caesar, and Caesar was jealous of Alexander, and Alexander was jealous of Zeus. And Zeus did not exist.

In other words, you can be the king of the world, as legendary as Caesar, and there will still be someone of whom you can be jealous.

That's why you have to let God love the need for comparison right out of you.

((((( )))))

So, if you find yourself checking in on Instagram and start to feel like a failure, remember that everything isn't always as it appears, and that comparison is a terrible trap.

You might feel you aren't good enough, but that is just a lie.

Here's the deal: You are not a mistake. You are a masterpiece. Don't let anyone tell you differently.

You might think yourself a bit dull and boring. But in God's eyes, you are far more interesting than you know. Psalm 139:17-18 says that God's thoughts toward you outnumber the grains of sand. Do you know how many that is? According to people who spend their time looking into such things, the earth has roughly 7.5 x 10 to the eighteenth power grains of sand, which equates to about seven quintillion, five hundred quadrillion grains.[2]

Um…that's quite a few.

It's a poetic way of saying that God can't take His mind off you. He is totally smitten.

Further, in that same psalm, David writes of God, "You knit me together in my mother's womb" (Psalm 139:13). Which means you were carefully crafted. You were planned and shaped and constructed to be one of God's masterpieces.

This means that there is nothing about you that is a result of chance. It's all artistry. Every one of the approximately 75 trillion cells in your body, each one containing hundreds of thousands of molecules. Every cell contains six feet of DNA containing more than 3 billion letters of coding. On top of that, you have 206 bones, countless proteins that collide with each other a billion times per second, and a brain with 100 billion interconnected neurons, each with ten thousand connections and synapses.

Does this make you wish you had paid more attention in your math and science classes?

Yes, we are something special; the creation of the Master Artist.

Each of us is unique. I have never heard a fish asking why bad things happen to good fish. Nor have I read a poem about love's trans-dimensional transcendence written by a velociraptor. We members of the human race are unique, made in the *imago Dei*, the image of God, capable of rationality and profundity as well as of creating awesome practical jokes and inventing the Disneyland churro!

So, when you are feeling crummy about who you are, you might just want to keep all this in mind.

((((( )))))

You are not a mistake. You are a miracle.

Don't waste a lot of energy propping up a false image to the world. You'll never be happy being fake, selling out, prostituting yourself for money, toeing the party line, trying to fit in, worrying too much about what others think, saying things you don't really believe, or projecting a false identity into the world. That's all a colossal waste of time and energy.

Don't apologize for not being what others expect you to be. Instead, be extreme about being *you*. Don't be scared or intimidated by the opinions of other people.

One of the reasons why depression got the best of me for so long was that I was expending a lot of energy playing a part. I was a teenage pastor trying to act out the role of the friendly neighborhood minister who didn't want to offend anyone and wanted everyone to be happy with me. Deep inside, though, I was a bit of a rebel. The last thing I wanted to do was to sit in an air-conditioned office and write emails in response to parishioners who were complaining about how loud the music was during Sunday worship.

I secretly wanted to do a handstand during the sermon.

What I discovered was that I could serve God a whole lot better by being Ben and staying in my own lane. I decided to be like Paul, who lived his life without worrying about being safe and acceptable. Here was a man who started a riot or a revival everywhere he went, who was shipwrecked and spent a day and a night in the sea, who got tossed in prison because he wouldn't stop talking about Jesus, who tangled with the authorities (both secular and religious), who was bitten by a deadly viper, who fought beasts in Ephesus, who was delivered out of the mouth of a lion, and who was the target of an angry religious mob who threw rocks at him and left him for dead.

Now that's really living.

The example of the apostle Paul was completely unlike what I found was expected of me as a young pastor. I was supposed to meet with people at Starbucks and talk about a lot of things that were ultimately kind of pointless, to repeat a bunch of religious clichés and one-liners from the pulpit, to answer a bunch of theological questions about stuff like whether we should store up canned goods for a post-tribulation rapture.

I was supposed to be someone I wasn't, and the result was a debilitating depression.

So, I ran in the other direction. Toward radical adventures with God, skateboarding to His glory, writing a fantasy trilogy, making movies with my friends, and traveling all over the world speaking passionately about a different approach to faith. Being, to capture it all in one word, an *optimisfit*.

Needless to say, I am much happier.

What about you? Whose script for your life are you trying to perform? The part that God wrote uniquely for you or some stock form of existence that keeps everybody happy...except you?

(((( ))))

In *One Flew Over the Cuckoo's Nest*, Ken Kesey tells the story about a man who had the courage to be himself—even if it meant rebelling against the system all by himself. There is no greater courage than being fearless enough to be yourself, utterly and unapologetically. Frankly, it's just about the rarest thing going.

Don't die as a pawn in someone else's game.

It's literally harmful to your psyche, as well as your happiness, to try to be someone else. It creates a cognitive dissonance, which means that your actions and behaviors don't line up with your true beliefs. It just isn't sustainable. It kills something at your very core. Something inside of you dies.

So, don't do what you don't believe in.

I try to approach even insignificant stuff from a place of conviction rather than convenience. I happen to believe that it is wrong to kill animals and eat them. Period. So, I am a vegetarian. In most of the circles where I run, I am ruthlessly trolled for this. My vegetarianism makes some people think I am secretly New Age or that I embrace some sort of Eastern philosophy. They love to razz me about it, but that's fine. I've been in many a debate about Peter's vision of the animals where God tells him, "Kill and eat" (Acts 10:13). My friends take it to mean we should have a carnivorous diet, whereas I think it's talking about Peter not calling the Gentiles unclean, as Jews did in that day. Honestly, though, the conversations never get heated. It's all in good fun.

Bottom line is that I've made the decision to never do anything I don't absolutely believe in.

That, I have found, is one of the chief secrets to real happiness.

Other people's armor is rarely a good fit. Just ask David.

·((((( )))))·

Don't accept the labels people put on you if they don't represent who you really are.

Labels shape our consciousness.

Among Polynesian tribes, there isn't a word for grief. They simply don't have a word to label that emotion. When someone dies, they say they "experience fatigue." They don't have the language for grief, so they evidently experience it as fatigue instead. You cannot feel that for which you don't have a name.

The ancient Greeks didn't have a word for blue. To them, the color didn't exist. They couldn't see it without a name for it. Instead, they spoke of the ocean as "the wine-dark sea."

We are only conscious of that which we label.

That is why it's essential that you don't let someone else label you. It's up to you to do the labeling. And God will help you find the best label for you.

If you don't know who you are anymore because other people have toyed with your head and branded you through unkind comments and vilifying nicknames, if you have been abused or had your name dragged through the mud, if you have been told only of your failures and limitations, then it's time to tear off the labels.

They only invite the unwanted guest of depression into our lives.

So, vent these deleterious emotions and get the catharsis you need in the presence of God and affirming friends. Don't let the cruel things others have said make you believe that you are who they say you are. Don't be held captive to their assessments.

You are not damaged goods. You are not a loser. You are not unlovable.

You are a beloved child of God.

He stands with you when others put their labels on you.

My friend, you are adored. You are so, so, so much loved. You don't need to work for that love. You do not need to be anything different to receive that love. In His eyes, you are the bomb.* You are His magnum opus, His tour de force, His piece de resistance, so settle into your skin. Be you.

---

* Except for this one, I have avoided using footnotes in this book. But I thought it would be fun to use at least one, so here it is! In reference to being the bomb, it's worth remembering that you contain the potential energy equivalent of 30 hydrogen bombs, so I am being quite literal. (Rob Bell, *What We Talk About When We Talk About God*, pages 54-55.) Now, wasn't that worth the effort of looking down here at the bottom of the page?

Let Him sign you as His masterpiece.

(((( ))))))

Jesus taught that the same God who numbers the stars also counts the hairs on your head (Matthew 10:30; Luke 12:7). It's been computed that the average blond person has 150,000 hairs, the average dark-haired person has 110,000 to 100,000 hairs, and the average redhead has 90,000 hairs.[3] God keeps track of each one. I wouldn't use this information to approach a girl and announce, "You have 93,437 hairs…I've been paying attention." She would be taillights for sure. She'd think I was obsessed. Well, God is that obsessed with you. So, the next time someone presses "dislike" on your video post, remember that God has already given you a thumbs-up on your value.

(((( ))))))

Jim Carrey once said, "Depression is your body saying…I don't want to be this character anymore. I don't want to hold up this avatar that you've created in the world. It's too much for me."[4] Which, frankly, is a lot of work and not at all worth the effort. Some people choose to disappear into the social woodwork and try to go unnoticed rather than living with the labels others want to put on them.

Sometimes we think we just want to disappear, but the truth is we really want to be found. We want to be discovered, explored, understood, appreciated, and loved.

We hide who we really are because we think that won't pass muster. We believe that if others know us as we are, then they won't like us much and won't think we are worthy of their attention and respect.

We apologize for our inability to be what others expect us to be.

We hide our true selves and put on masks. We pretend to be something we are not. Maybe we can fool people into thinking we fit in.

We don't dare let anyone see the person we really are.

And when we live like this, we are going to be miserable inside. We try to maintain that false identity. We slip on a more acceptable mask. And it does such damage to who we truly are. It isn't easy to deal with the cognitive dissonance of pretending. Our truest self suffocates under all the layers of pretense.

Jim Carrey was right. This is a recipe for depression.

(((( )))))

So here is my recipe for moving out of this whirlpool of false identity and mask wearing. Three simple, uncomplicated words to coax you out of this depression-inducing syndrome and into a better relationship with the real you:

Own.

Your.

Oddness.

(((( )))))

Back in Bible times, it was thought to be a curse to be left handed. Only three lefties are specifically mentioned in the Bible, and they all came from the tribe of Benjamin.

Benjamin's name, interestingly enough, means "son of my right hand." So, oddly, all the southpaws were from the right-handed tribe. Make of that what you will...

Well, one of these southpaws was named Ehud, and he was a great hero to his people. He was responsible for assassinating an evil king who was making everyone's lives miserable. What makes the story especially interesting is how he pulled it off. It was possible because he was left handed. Back then, in order to get into the presence of the king, the palace guard would frisk someone's left hip because the normal right-handed person would wear their weapon on that side, drawing their sword from across their body. Because most people were right-handed and the lefties were considered cursed, they weren't very careful about checking the right side. Ehud was able to slip past the palace guards without getting caught. His oddness was his asset, and he was able to get into the presence of the king.

The king in question was named Eglon, and he had the baddest of reputations (and not bad in a good way!). The Bible always tells it like it is, and what it tells us about Eglon is that he was a *very fat* man. Not someone who needed to shed a few extra pounds of fat but grossly overweight. Think Jabba the Hut from *Return of the Jedi*. He was so overweight that he likely had his own zip code. When someone told him he should exercise, he thought they were suggesting extra fries. Because the body is a temple, he said, "Why not add on some additions?" You get the idea, right?

So, Ehud strode bravely into the presence of the king, pulled his sword from his right side, and thrust it into the gut of Eglon. When he did, the sword disappeared into the fat. I mean, it was engulfed in the flabby fatness of the king. Perhaps this detail helps you understand why this is one of my favorite Bible stories (Judges 3:12-29).

Ehud lost his sword but won the battle. His curse became his glory. The southpaw used his left hand to win a victory for his people that day.

(((( ))))

Like Ehud, our oddness can be our glory. Our weakness can be our strength.

Though only 10 percent of the population today is made up of the left-handed, they seem to have a bit of advantage when it comes to the world of politics. "No fewer than six of 13 U.S. presidents since World War II have been lefties...[James Garfield] was also the first known southpaw to occupy the Oval Office. In addition to being ambidextrous...Garfield also spoke and wrote several different languages. His talents were so celebrated that people said he could write a sentence in Latin with one hand while simultaneously writing the same sentence in Greek with the other."[5]

Our oddness comes from God. The very thing that makes you *different* can help you make a *difference*. The thing that prevents you from *fitting in* empowers you to *stand out*. Your weakness may help others find victory.

Consider the fact that ex-drunks are usually the ones who start up AA meetings.

We help others most potently where we have suffered most poignantly. Our hurts become our superpowers. Our flaws become our defining glories.

My own flirtation with darkness when I was in the midst of deepest depression has led me to focus on hope as my message. Because I fought that fight, I can help others take up arms against their own depression.

Your scars can become your stars.

((((( )))))

People might be impressed with you because of your strengths, but they connect with you because of your weaknesses.

A significant element of my ministry is helping people who feel like they just can't go on. At heart I'm part of an anti-suicide movement.

Everything I've been through has given me the message I have today. If you look at the course of my life, I'm about the last person you'd think would be doing this. Somehow this kid from a pint-sized town seized on his giant-sized dreams, and God made them come true. But not before having to face down a lot of criticism and misunderstanding as well as all the pain of life. I've experienced people who said my speaking didn't compare with my dad (I don't blame them), been picketed by a crazy guy, had someone start up a Ben Courson hate group to attack my ministry, had people fall asleep during my talks and walk out on my speeches. I had to decide I was not going to try to please everyone around me, but that I was just going to focus on pleasing God. And I let Him use my oddness as an exclamation point on my message.

God wants to take you, oddness and all, and use you for His own purposes. Your oddness and shame can become your glory. Your crazy dreams can become the thing that takes you to your next level.

So…

Own.

Your.

Oddness.

WEAPON #7:
FRIENDVENTURES

You can't go it alone.

And you shouldn't be trying to.

I realize that for some of my readers, this is the place where I am expected to wax eloquent on how my faith has saved me. That God stepped in and made all the difference. Well, that is quite true…but my road to healing took a very different, and much wilder, course than I ever expected.

In the decade I experienced my fiercest battle with depression, I felt as if I were a gasoline engine into whose tank someone had poured several gallons of diesel. I was misfiring and sputtering and making little progress. I was disoriented. I was always tired. I wasn't so much moving through time as time was moving through me. I was a young man, but felt as if I were inside the soul of an unhappy senior citizen.

Ultimately, I found my healing in unexpected places.

Not in a church service, a healing revival meeting, an intervention, or a prayer circle.

Healing didn't come when people had deep talks with me, or invited me to coffee, or got on their knees with me. It happened when a crazy group of optimisfits showed up and reminded me that life could be fun again by embracing a childlike joy. It happened when they taught me how to throw a real party—not a pity party.

((((( )))))

Healing came because Sean invited me to go on a midnight run on a foggy night. I watched him as he jogged along, his floppy hair bouncing as he ran beside me. Then, tired, we jumped on a moving train to see where it might be headed.

Healing came because Cameron, who lives five hours away, texted me and asked if I wanted to grab something to eat from Del Taco. Then he texted "Ding Dong." Sure enough, I heard a knock at the door. He had traveled all that distance to arrive unannounced, just to eat tacos with me.

Healing came because Chase, a star receiver for UCLA, grabbed his skateboard and took me with him on an adventure in the aisles of Food for Less with our boards, humungous stuffed animals perched on our shoulders. A little innocent mayhem can be just the ticket for feeling blue.

Healing came because my friend Kellin, a rock star who knows what it is like to live on airplanes, laughed with me and helped me learn to say no when I felt burned out from living on the road. I'd been accepting way too many speaking engagements for far too long.

Healing came because Michael the drummer, Bo the vlogger, and Brooke the skater invented a game of football that could be played on skateboards. I'm not sure it'll catch on or become a professional sport, but I loved it. I joined wholeheartedly in the revelry.

Healing came because my buddies Cam and JoJo showed up at my house with an old-fashioned ghetto blaster and blasted the worst possible boy band songs as we made up the ugliest possible dance routines to accompany the music.

Healing came because my friend Cambria, who is a legitimate YouTube celebrity and now an author in her own right, knows how to smile away all my worries. If you could bottle up her enthusiastic positivity, it might just be the cure for most of the ills of this world. Her warm countenance said more than any words every could.

Healing came because I got to know an amazing singer-songwriter named Ryan Stevenson, who has blown everyone away with his song "The Eye of the Storm." The song reminds me I'm never, ever alone in my struggles; that the storm cannot take me where God cannot keep me. Jesus only did three things in storms: slept during them, stomped on them, or sternly rebuked them. His love surrounds me in the eye of the storm. If you don't know the song, check it out. I guarantee it'll do you good.

Healing came when my friend Christina, who has been seen by millions of people on TikTok, blasted punk songs in my Jeep as we expertly riffed on our air guitars.

Healing came when Cody, the fifth-ranked scooter rider in the world, visited Bilbo's Hobbit hole in New Zealand with me, and then ran with me through the Shire screaming "Gandalf" at the top of our lungs.

Healing came when Michael and Gracie sat with me beside a trio of waterfalls in a forest lit only by glow worms.

These are some of the people who have made a difference in my life, and if you take a minute to think about it, maybe you can identify your own squad. And if you don't have a squad, getting one should be at the top of your list of priorities.

Most of my friends are about the smartest people you could imagine, leaders in their fields and world experts. But as much as I value their talent, it's their ability to laugh that I cherish the most. All of them have a sense of humor. Believe me, I need that.

So do you.

(((( ))))

Pick your friends wisely, because they will either help make you a success at life or get in your way when you are trying to achieve your best. Did you know that Thomas Edison, Harry Firestone, and Henry Ford all had summer houses in the same neighborhood in Florida? These were dreamers associating with dreamers. Creativity flocks together.

Spirits are transferable. The Bible says that Daniel had an excellent spirit because he hung out with Shadrach, Meshach, and Abednego, each of whom was also described as having an excellent spirit. We become like our friends.

And if you have the kind of friends who make you feel worse about yourself whenever you are around them, then maybe it's time for a new crew.

If you run with skunks, you're gonna end up smelling like one.

If your friends are the equivalent of Larry, Curly, and Moe…well, good luck with that.

But if you hang out with friends who are optimisfits, you'll catch the contagion of laughter and hope. As Proverbs 27:17 reminds us, "As iron sharpens iron, so one man sharpens another." Your squad will not only sharpen you, but also help you battle against darkness and depression.

(((( ))))

My band of optimisfit friends and I recently decided that the best way to celebrate the New Year was to undertake an adventure—or a "friendventure" as we like to call them. We crowded into my Jeep like clowns in a clown car and drove up into the woods to do some exploring. What we saw was a reminder that God is the greatest artist of all.

The woods were enchanted, so we let our imaginations wander among the wonders. We floated through God's creation, breathing in the sky and listening to the roaring waterfalls. It felt as though the trees might break into a dance at any moment if we turned our back on them.

George MacDonald warned us not to sabotage or deconstruct nature through microscopes and science, but to let its beauty have its way with us. Instead of analyzing and dissecting it to try to understand what you are seeing, he suggested, you should just let the magic of God's world wash over you. G.K. Chesterton encouraged his readers to be childlike in the face of nature and compared the created world to a toy that we should play with. He knew that when children take their toys apart to try to see what makes them work, it ruins part of the fun. Just play about in the cosmos "as is." Remember, when you tear apart that toy to examine it more closely, it never works the way it used to when you try to put it back together. You just need to let it be and enjoy it for what it is. The created world is the same way.

I've already told you how much I love science, but sometimes you just need to step back and let things be. Let the universe move you by its beauty without worrying about understanding it all. Let the mystery be. As fascinating as quantum theory is, sometimes you just have to put away the lab coat and the microscope and cease from breaking things down to their elemental particles for study. Instead, enjoy the magic right before your eyes.

So, my squad and I celebrated the New Year in the best possible way—with childlike joy, narwhals, owls, zebra pigs, and the like. (As well as an arsenal of Nerf rifles for good measure.)

The whole experience was another reminder that my tribe of friends was a big factor in mending my depression. If you want to find healing, maybe what you need isn't another deep conversation or a session of intense existential navel gazing. Maybe what you need is just God and your squad.

Part of the solution for my blues can be to party with my friends in an enchanted setting—the beauty of nature, some Nerf guns, a lot of craziness, and the magic of shared love. Just the thing for a New Year... and a new you!

(((( ))))

When we become depressed, especially if the depression is partly caused by someone hurting us, it's easy for us to withdraw into our own little world. We think we want to disappear, but the reality is we just want to be found.

Being isolated is never good for our psyche. God didn't make us to travel through life alone. We need other people.

The Bible tells us that one can put to flight a thousand, but two can put to flight ten thousand (Deuteronomy 32:30). Two are, by this biblical math, *ten times* more powerful than one! We are exponentially more effective when we take on a friend to help us battle the dark places in our lives.

Paul encourages us to take up the shield of faith (Ephesians 6:16). In ancient Rome, shields were constructed so that they could interlock with the shields of other warriors, thereby creating one massive makeshift barricade. When needed, the soldiers could march on their enemy like an impregnable moving wall. So, maybe taking up your shield isn't only about providing protection for yourself, but about linking up with others to march on your enemy.

The path to victory is this: When you feel like giving up, it just means it's time to squad up!

When Jesus wanted to spread the good news of His Kingdom, He gathered a group of disciples and followers. He had a posse, an entourage.

Shouldn't we follow His example?

((((( )))))

My friends have taught me how to hope. They have modeled the meaning of life, which is, essentially, enjoying the joy of being enjoyed by God. God does not endure you. He does not put up with you. He doesn't wince at the thought of spending time with you. Zephaniah 3:17 says He rejoices over you with singing. You are at the top of His Spotify playlist, and He loves to sing your song!

((((( )))))

My friends also taught me that I shouldn't always be living in my head, which is a very real temptation for yours truly. They've shown me how to live from my heart. That might be the greatest gift of all.

Don't get me wrong. My friends aren't always filled with joy and happiness. They have their own issues with depression and suicidal thoughts. But they have also chosen to be dead serious about not being overly serious. They have taught me how to rise up from the ashes; to let depression be a teacher…but not a master.

((((( )))))

It's part of my nature to crave time alone. A little solo time now and then is healthy. But don't withdraw. Drawing the shades, climbing into bed, and putting on sad music isn't the vibe that is going to help. You need your friends. You need your squad.

If you want to go fast, go alone.

If you want to go far, go together.

Loneliness, according to one scientific study, is akin to smoking a pack of cigarettes every day.[1] That's how unhealthy it is for you.

So, even when I don't want to, I need to spend time with my peeps.

(((( )))))

Is there someone you should call right now?

14

WEAPON #8: HEAVEN

As I sit down to write this chapter, I am struggling.

My beautiful brother, Peter-John Courson, just ten years older than me, went to heaven yesterday.

Already I miss him more than I can say.

I can't stop crying…

((((( )))))

Consider this chapter an act of catharsis on my part. A journal of my thoughts in the face of this loss.

Peter, I am grasping at straws and groping in the dark to take this all in, frantically searching to make some sense out of how you could have left this world so young and with so much of your life seemingly left unfinished. I'm not sure I was ever able to fully process our sister's death, and I don't really know what to do with yours.

((((( )))))

During the last minutes of your life, Peter, I stood by your bedside as you took your final breaths. I looked into your endlessly blue eyes and saw through them a window into another world. You were lying there straddling between two realities—this one and the next. It seemed as though something inside you was already escaping into that other dimension.

Cancer wracked your body with pain, but your lungs and heart were still fighting off the disease with all their might. Your chest heaved as though you were a runner on the last legs of a marathon, so very close to the finish line.

You couldn't speak, but your labored breathing mirrored the words of an aging apostle Paul: "I have fought the good fight, I have finished the race" (2 Timothy 4:7).

Just like him, Pete, you ran so well. So gloriously well.

But your time came too soon.

During the last hour of your life, Dad looked over at me from the other side of the bed and spoke softly. I'm not sure you were conscious enough to hear him, but I hoped you could. He was pointing out that the song which was quietly playing on the radio near the bed was "Take My Hand and Walk" by the Kry. Right there, at the end of your beautiful life, the same song was playing that we had listened to during the memorial service for our beloved sister Jessie.

The same hand that walked Jessie down the aisle was now reaching out for you. Her homecoming song was yours too.

The rabbis of old got it right. What we humans call coincidence is just God wishing to remain anonymous.

I'll always remember how your mouth was open so shockingly wide as you struggled to catch your final breaths. And then, when you passed, it wasn't that you died so much as that you were…released.

The spirit inside you just got up and left the room. You went to another place.

J.R.R. Tolkien wrote, "There is a place called 'heaven' where the good here unfinished is completed; and where the stories unwritten, and hopes unfulfilled, are continued."

And then he concluded: "We may laugh together yet."

That is my confidence.

That is my relentless hope.

This sorrow will be turned to joy.

We will laugh together once again.

I believe.

But right now, Pete, I cannot hold back the tears.

((((( )))))

I won't soon forget these lines from William Wordsworth:

> Our birth is but a sleep and a forgetting;
> The Soul that rises with us, our life's Star,
> Hath had elsewhere its setting
> And cometh from afar;
> Not in entire forgetfulness,
> And not in utter nakedness,
> But trailing clouds of glory do we come
> From God, who is our home.

((((( )))))

My family has known a lot of pain from the deaths of our loved ones. My dad's first wife died in a car accident, leaving three kids behind. Then Jessie died in an accident in her VW bug while she was still in high school. Now my brother, at an age that should have been the prime of his life, died after battling Crohn's disease for 20 years.

Me, I suffered for ten years with clinical depression. I was suicidal. And I got blindsided by a romantic heartbreak that put a sudden and unexpected end to an eight-year relationship.

And you can add to all these things the constant stress that arises from a mentally unstable man in our community who has made it his personal mission to take my family down. He follows my dad and me to our speaking engagements and holds up a handwritten sign that accuses us of being hypocritical and even criminal. He contacts radio and TV stations, and writes letters to accuse us falsely in order to ruin our ministries. He warned my publisher against printing my book. To this day it still isn't clear why he has settled all his hate and malice upon us. He's been doing this ever since I was a kid.

In my short lifetime, I feel as though I've experienced enough pain for three long lives.

So, as you consider my words about hope—about a relentless optimism in the face of all the fear and pain and confusion of life—remember that my words come from a place of hope in the face of the worst kinds of pain.

My pain has not broken me…though it has tried to.

And the death of Peter-John won't break me either.

(((( )))))

God can take our hurt and our pain and use it to craft us into greater people.

Edward Elgar was one of the greatest English composers and most famous for his "Pomp and Circumstance," which is played during every graduation ceremony you've ever attended. As William Barclay tells it, once Elgar was listening "to a young girl singing a solo from one of his works. She had a voice of exceptional purity and clarity and range, and almost perfect technique." But Elgar sensed something missing in her performance. "When she had finished, Sir Edward said softly: 'She will be really great when something happens to break her heart.'"[1]

Truly, our heartbreaks can be fuel for greatness.

More than ever, I am determined to give my life to hope, to experience what C.S. Lewis called "the gaiety of battle," and to be swept up into my role in the great epic story of which I am called to be a part.

Sometimes meaning comes most clearly and directly through fighting bravely and recklessly against the tyranny of despair that is arrayed against us. With our sword of faith, with the strength of our convictions, we muster our courage in the face of death—whether our own or someone we love.

As my brother Peter once said:

"Life is short, but so are our trials and tribulations."

Take it from one who knew.

((((( )))))

Ever since the death of my brother, I've been thinking a lot about heaven. And about how that hope can make a difference for us as we struggle to make sense of the loss of someone we love. I'd like to share with you five reasons we can hold on to hope and know that the best is yet to come.

First, I believe in life after death because of what I have learned from the theory of quantum mechanics. According to this scientific paradigm, information is indestructible. It might change shape, but it can never be lost. For example, you could burn a piece of paper and it will become a pile of ashes. If you did this, you could still theoretically read the information in the atoms and molecules of that ash and see that it was once a love note or a receipt from Walmart. It's all there, but it's in an entirely new form.

Hypothetically, one could trace all the information contained in that pile all the way back to the very beginning and origin of the universe itself. Nothing is lost. Nothing is wasted. It was all there back at the moment of singularity when everything first came into being.

Our bodies are a flurry of dancing atoms. And all those particles are part of the giant recycling project of the universe. Some people believe we are nothing more than the sum total of our body parts—eyelashes, belly button, toenails—and that when we are buried in the ground after we die, we are recycled into coal that future humans will dig out from the earth and use to stoke the fire of some factory. That our destiny is to float out of a chimney and into the ether some millions of years from now.

But contemporary science is offering another view. It tells us that matter cannot be created or destroyed, and that all subatomic particles are relationships of energy. You can't destroy matter. You can only rearrange its atomic structure.

So, when a parent says to their teenager who has just engaged in some random unrecommended stunt, "You think you are indestructible, don't you?"—the technical answer is that, "Yes, as a matter of fact, I am!"

Jesus told His disciples that "whoever lives and believes in Me shall never die. Do you believe this?" (John 11:26 NKJV).

Ultimately, you can't die. The *you* that is you is more than the sum of your knowable parts. Just as a novel is more than its words and a song more than mere notes, so you're more than a collection of particles and atoms and cells and molecules.

((((( )))))

Second, our souls are hardwired for eternity. Ecclesiastes tells us that "He has also set eternity in the human heart" (Ecclesiastes 3:11).

Throughout the entire history of human beings, people have believed in an afterlife; that there is *something more* beyond the boundaries of this world. Science validates this. Even in secularized cultures where belief in God is relatively low, belief in the afterlife or some persistence of consciousness beyond death maintains majority support.

Why is this belief so common and so universal? Is it perhaps because, as Ecclesiastes tells us, God has put eternity in our hearts?

Several years ago, when Pete was undergoing brain surgery, he was given a glimpse of heaven. I love his description of what heaven was like. His phrase: "Fun, with meaning." He never doubted for a second the reality of what he had experienced, and it was this vision that gave him such strength in the face of his own death.

((((( )))))

Third, I believe in the afterlife because love demonstrates the immortality of the soul. "Many waters cannot quench love; rivers cannot sweep it away" (Song of Songs 8:7). Love, in other words, cannot die. Think about this: We still feel a deep love for many who are no longer with us. There is no social utility for such conviction, no Darwinian explanation, no evolutionary principle that would explain why we continue to love those whom we've lost to death. We love in the present tense those who died in the past. This kind of continuance of love is a powerful metaphysical argument for the immortality of the soul.

We may die, but our soul will live on.

So we, as ones whose hope is in the God of hope, do not mourn as the world mourns. We hurt, but we hurt with hope. And one day our mourning will be turned to dancing (Psalm 30:11 NKJV).

We can't see heaven, but we can see graves. And yet our sight is faulty and not always to be trusted. Science now tells us that much of what we see is an atomic illusion of rapidly moving particles. We are tricked into seeing solidity that isn't there.

Our faith is the *substance* of things hoped for (Hebrews 11:1), and the valley of death is only a *shadow* (Psalm 23:4). Would you rather get hit by a semitruck or a semitruck's shadow?

Hope, my friends, is substantive.

Death? It's only a shadow.

(((((   )))))

Fourth, I believe I will see Pete again because of the etymological meaning of the word "breath." In both Greek and Hebrew, the words for "breath" and "spirit" are the same word. And Genesis 2:7 points out how we were created: "The LORD God formed a man from the dust of the ground and breathed into his nostrils the breath of life, and the man became a living being." Breath creates breath.

At the end, Pete was panting like a runner, and every single breath was a struggle. My dad gently placed his hand on Pete and said, "You've finished the race. Just let go." I cannot help but tear up as I remember this sacred moment.

When Pete stopped breathing, it was as though his spirit was released. And he left the room. His body was still there, but the essential reality that is Pete had exited the scene.

He was there.

Then he wasn't.

The nurse whose job it was to be with Pete as he died had been present for many deaths. It was what she did for a living. She told me that her experiences with the dying have made her totally unafraid of death because it's not so much that people's lives are terminated as that they fly away. The body is still there, but the person isn't there anymore.

((((( ))))))

Fifth, God has put within each of us a desire to be in the winner's circle. Humans seem to have an innate and inherent need to associate with winners. We love to drop the names of famous folk we've met as though that somehow gives more validity to our own existence. It's why we wear the jerseys of our favorite sporting teams or the swag of our favorite bands. We want to be part of something that is victorious. The band Queen liked to belt out "We Are the Champions," and everyone in the audience would pump their fists and raise their hands in triumph. We all like to think of ourselves as winners.

Over the years I have often donned a Yankees ballcap. Why? Because they are winners. When I was recently looking through the family album, I saw that Pete frequently wore just such a cap himself.

Ever notice that when your favorite team is victorious that you say, "*We* won!" Or when your team loses that you say, "*They* lost!" Notice the change in pronoun? We love to associate ourselves with winners.

When it comes to death, the victory is ours.

The Bible tells us that death is the final foe to be defeated, and the battle belongs to the Lord. He has an undefeated record. He's the One you want to team up with.

The apostle Paul wrote,

> When the perishable has been clothed with the imperishable, and the mortal with immortality, then the saying that is written will come true: "Death has been swallowed up in victory."
>
> "Where, O death, is your victory? Where, O death, is your sting?"
>
> The sting of death is sin, and the power of sin is the law. But thanks be to God! He gives us the victory through our Lord Jesus Christ (1 Corinthians 15:54-57).

The word for "victory" in Greek that Paul uses here is *nike*. We are on the winning team because we have the Nike swoosh stitched to our spirits. Death will not have the last word. That word belongs to God. And that word is *nike*. That word is victory.

((((( )))))

According to Jewish custom, it was proper for a person to own a tomb. But the purchase of a tomb was a significant expense. Jesus, though, didn't bother to buy a tomb for Himself. Evidently, He was a good businessman. Why on earth would He purchase something He was only planning to borrow for three days? He borrowed the tomb so that God could buy you.

The final message about death is this: There is an empty tomb.

15

WEAPON #9: EL ROI

Sometimes even the best of friends will not be able to help you move past your bondage to depression. Sometimes you need the kind of help that comes from someone with expertise in how our emotions and brain chemistry work.

I remember when I had sunk to the lowest point in my depression, when it felt as though some demon from hell had taken a nefarious lighter from the underworld and set my brain on fire. I was tormented by dark thoughts and even darker feelings. I even imagined I could see witches laughing at me, their distorted faces twisted, their voices cackling, and their eyes leering at me with evil intent.

Umm…this is kind of what mental illness can look like. And it isn't pretty.

Those of you who've gone through severe depression might be able to relate. Your mind gets so twisted up that reality can be distorted. Which only makes you feel more helpless.

If you've never been down this road, perhaps a glimpse inside what I was going through might be instructive. If nothing else, maybe it will give you some insight that will be helpful for friends or family who are locked in a battle right now.

If you're currently struggling with depression, then let this be a reminder that you aren't the first person who ever felt this way. Believe me, I understand what you are going through.

((((( )))))

First, let's get something out of the way right now. There are those who say suicide is a selfish option. Well, that just isn't true. In the moment you are considering the option of killing yourself, you can almost feel like it is an altruistic act. You feel like you are a burden to everyone around you, and you're doing them a favor by removing yourself from their lives. You know your loved ones will be sad and mourn your death for a while, but you imagine they'll get over it soon enough. And in the long run they'll be better off without having to deal with you and your problems.

Second, a common misconception is that people who threaten to commit suicide are just making a bid for attention. To which I answer, so what if they are? We all want to be seen and understood and known. If someone needs attention so badly that they are talking about killing themselves, that isn't a cause for shame. It's just a sign of how alone they feel in their pain and struggle. They feel like Hagar did, dying alone in the wilderness without a sign of help. Thankfully, God did not leave her in the struggle. He revealed Himself as "El Roi," which means, "the God who sees" (Genesis 16:13). God saw Hagar. He sees you. And He doesn't want to leave anyone to suffer alone.

So, why does someone want to commit suicide?

I think it's usually because the mental and emotional agony feels like too much to bear. I'm sure many readers have at some point experienced such intense *physical* pain—even if only for a short time—that dying seemed better than continuing to endure it.

A few months ago I contracted a food toxin on a long plane flight, and after we landed EMTs had to cart me off the plane and put me into an ambulance. When I finally was out of the woods, I still felt terribly ill. Driving away from the hospital, I had to pull off the road, my stomach churning in agony. I hunched over on my hands and knees by the side of the road, violently throwing up. I had to stop and repeat this procedure several times on the way to the house where I was staying. I was hit so hard by the illness that it lasted for a week. I was in such agony from the poisoning that I just wanted to die. It seemed too excruciating to bear. Anything, I thought at the time, not to feel this way anymore.

Well, it's not much different when the pain is psychological and emotional rather than physical. Rational thought goes out the window, and the darkest options open up before you. You're not thinking logically anymore. You are flirting with darkness. You are only surviving on the level of pure animal suffering. In fact, neurobiology reveals that the intense feelings of self-rejection and emotional hurt can actually be registered in the brain *as* physical suffering.[1]

((((( )))))

That's how it felt to me at one point in my life. *Of course, I didn't want to live any longer.* Why would I want to prolong the pain? The ground disappeared underneath me, and I felt as though I was falling through a psychic space—a hideous free fall of dark consciousness. I couldn't sleep, and if by chance I did fall asleep for a while, I would awake in the darkness during the middle of the night when all rational thought seems impossible and be overcome with unhappiness. Sometimes I got headaches that made my temples throb without relief.

My depression was making me physically ill.

Nothing brought me pleasure. Food didn't taste good, and I didn't want to eat anyway. I didn't want to do any of the things I normally loved, like listening to music. Nothing brought me joy. My only reality was how much I hurt.

I had frequent and uncontrollable panic attacks. They would seize me at unexpected moments, and I could never anticipate when the next one might hit. I began to panic over the fact that I might panic at any moment. Sometimes I'd be driving my Jeep down the road and would have to pull over and sob, hyperventilating and unable to catch the next breath. My brain dreamt up horrors I couldn't see but which filled me with fear.

Sometimes it was just easier to stay in bed, hiding under the covers.

So, I considered various methods for killing myself. At one point I convinced myself that putting a plastic bag over my head would be the best option. It would at least stifle my psychic scream of pain.

For a time, I became addicted to watching horror films, especially the ones with supernatural themes. The stories about tormenting demons seemed real to me, just like what I was going through. They were oddly cathartic. They mirrored the strange things that swam in the depths of my subconscious. They reflected the orc dungeon in which I had found myself chained.

((((( )))))

My heart was sick. It seemed like this was not just a physical or psychological war I was fighting but a spiritual one. It's no wonder that the line between mental illness and demonic possession is seemingly such a thin one in the Bible. My own mental illness felt a lot like what I would imagine demon possession to be like.

I had no confidence I would ever get any better or that anything would change in my psyche.

I had nothing to live for.

What is worse is that I was doing all the right things. I was eating as clean as Tom Brady, praying passionately, studying how the brain worked in some hope I could find help there, and exercising every day. I even had a good group of friends, though none of them could really understand what I was going through.

Finally, I realized I need more than all these good things.

I needed help.

Professional help.

(((( ))))

For some fundamentalist Christians, the whole topic of counseling, therapy, and medication can be controversial. Some might not like what I'm going to say, but I'm going to say it anyway because I have earned the right through my own experience. So, here goes…

A few earnest prayers and Bible verses aren't going to be enough to get most people past their own flirtation with darkness. Well-meaning people might tell you that the solution to your problem is right there in the Bible, but I'm here to say that it's more complicated than that. Biblical counselors may be able to provide some relief to people with mild cases of depression, but when you are in psychological pain, you'll need more than a spiritual Band-Aid.

And that is perfectly okay.

(((( ))))

When my sister died, I grieved and moved on, allowing myself a week or two of mourning. After all, she was in heaven. So, I just kept going. When I had a traumatic romantic heartbreak, I didn't stop to suffer. Again, I just pushed it all down inside and kept going. Then my brother died. Once again, I didn't stop to deal with the pain. I just kept speaking and traveling and being a leader. And the suicidal level of depression just kept gnawing at me as I tried to follow my ministry goals.

Don't get me wrong. I'm kind of proud that I didn't give up. Sometimes work and distraction and a little escapism are good things. The problem is, when you bury your grief and keep working toward your career goals without working on your feelings, grief will eventually bury you. The trauma just continued to pile up on me, the result of an avalanche of emotions that hadn't really been addressed.

It was time to get some serious help.

((((( )))))

Going to see a counselor was a big leap for me. Frankly, I've always been a little bit suspicious of psychology. I'm skeptical about Freud's theories of infantile sexuality (go ahead and Google that if you must!), Jungian dream analysis, Adler's inferiority complex, the ever-popular Enneagram, and so many other schools of psychological thought. All these ideas are kind of intriguing, but it seems to me that human beings can't so easily be reduced to their various formulations. There's just so much speculation going on.

Meanwhile, the psychological community continues to prescribe antidepressants as though they are some kind of candy—throwing darts in the dark at the problem without using brain scans. C'mon, Doc. I'm looking for a little science here.

Years ago, my earlier experience with a therapist didn't go so well. He referred to me as "Little Ben" and attempted a Freudian analysis of my situation. Little did he know that I'd read up on all the techniques he was trying to use on me—so I was always one step ahead of him. When the sessions were over, I came away from this experience feeling judged and manipulated and not helped a bit. My counselor was a good man, but it wasn't a good fit. So I skateboarded away and swore off counseling for good.

At least so I thought.

Then, years later, at the urging of my sister, who knew me well enough to see through my bravado to the pain that was raging below the surface, I tried again. I was leery, but I knew I needed something. I was *desperate*.

That's when I started my sessions with Megan. She was a therapist who started to make a difference in my life when she got me talking about what was really going on deep below the surface. Her "talking cure" helped me stop suppressing my emotions and get honest with myself about how torn up I was inside. I'd read enough about mental health to understand that when our emotions are given breathing room, that affects everything—our physical, emotional, and intellectual performance.

In her presence I could breathe. I could slow down and lift the rug under which I'd hidden all the trauma. I could control the hyperventilating that would often follow some of my best sermons. I could name the anxiety because she had diagnosed me as suffering from complex PTSD. Wouldn't you know it? I couldn't settle for regular old PTSD. I had to suffer from the *complex* variety! With her help, I could drag the hidden hurts out into the open and finally shine a brilliant light into the dark places and deep shadows of my mind. Megan assured me that the very act of wrestling through my issues was a form of prayer.

It was cathartic.

It was healing.

I felt a little like Job. After all he'd been through, he sat in the ashes for seven days and seven nights, saying nothing.

Just processing…

((((( )))))

If you don't sit with your pain, it will eventually rear its ugly, leviathan head. You've gotta deal with it. Which is why, in my opinion, engaging in some sort of therapy would be a good idea for every pastor. If you never process the burdens that fester inside, your subconscious is going to bring them to the surface in ways you can't plan for. Your unhealthy emotions, attitudes, and secret struggles will invade your ministry and even show up in your sermons. That's why it is critical that you stay on a healthy path.

If all this sounds like a bunch of psychobabble to you, then I'm sorry.

But guess what? Counseling began to make a huge difference in my life.

((((( )))))

I started to process the feelings I'd dug out from deep inside me. I sat with my pain.

Pain isn't meant to be *suppressed* but *expressed*. In the Western world we usually keep our grief to ourselves or sometimes allow for a single sexy tear to drift down our face to mark our sorrow. We may apologize if we weep too much after the death of a family member, as though keeping it all together and putting on a good face is the best way to deal with the pain. In the Middle East they know better. They wail at their funerals. They aren't afraid of a little ugly crying, the kind of bawling your eyes out that causes the makeup to run. They set aside 40 days to mourn.

Megan didn't sit there and tell me everything was okay and to keep a stiff upper lip. She let me unleash the torrents of tears that had dammed up behind all the suppressed emotions. This, I learned, is the essential first step to healing, and you've got to do it. You've gotta let it all out.

Otherwise, you will eventually pay a big price.

I was tired of shelling out for my agony. Maybe you are too. Maybe it's time for you to get some help too.

Not all counseling methods are equally effective, but if you make the effort to find a good therapist, it might start you on the road to healing.

There are some things you just can't do by yourself.

One is table tennis.

Getting your emotions healed is another.

(((( ))))

After the resurrection, Jesus waited for the disciples at the Sea of Galilee (John 21). On the shore He made breakfast over a charcoal fire, similar to the charcoal fire on the night when Peter denied knowing Him. Jesus asked Peter three times: "Do you love me?" just as Peter had denied Him three times. This powerful moment strikes me as an anticipation of the modern psychological technique of the psychodrama. Let's face it, Jesus was a master therapist.

(((( ))))

The apostle Peter reminded believers that they can cast their cares upon Him (1 Peter 5:7).

The apostle Paul offers a further recommendation: that we "*carry each other's burdens*" (Galatians 6:2, emphasis added).

Counseling is a great way to unload our own burdens and let someone else help us carry them.

((((( )))))

One important element of therapy is getting help to realize you might need more than a series of conversations with your counselor. You might also need some medicine.

There's no shame in that. I'm no expert on psychotropic drugs and anti-depressants, but I know they are an important component of getting well for a lot of people. I've done a great deal of research, and many people swear by their effectiveness. Experts still don't know entirely how they work, and some people allege they are just placebos, but in the pioneering stages of this experimental science, it's important to keep an open mind.

Like a parachute, the mind doesn't work unless it is open.

When Paul headed out on some of his missionary journeys, he brought along Luke, who was a physician. Even though Paul could bring about supernatural healing by prayer, cast out demons, and even shake off poisonous snakes, he was a practical guy. According to Acts 19:11-12, he even transferred his healing power through handkerchiefs and aprons. Yet Paul chose a doctor for one of his companions. That same doctor was the author of one of the Gospels. Clearly Paul had no problem with the medical community. Neither did Jesus.

When Jesus healed a man by using spit, He was using a method that was believed in His day to have medicinal value. The Roman historian Tacitus tells us that the emperor Vespasian once healed a man with his spit.[2] Whether or not we believe that Tacitus got the facts right, it shows that the ancients believed that spit had medical powers. Even today, when you think about it, what is the first thing we do when we cut or burn our finger? We put it in our mouth to soothe the pain. So, maybe Jesus was making a positive nod to medical science in His day.

My point is that natural help and spiritual help aren't mutually exclusive options. It's not an either/or. We can combine the homeopathy of the East with the pharmacology of the West. Prayers and pills can work together to make you feel better.

If someone has an infection, what do they do? They take an antibiotic.

If someone has something going wrong in their brain chemistry, what do they do? Just pray it away? Or do they address it with an antidepressant? Medical studies are showing more clearly all the time that depression is not only a response to your environment but also often has a biological component. I'm not advocating for a *Brave New World* or popping pills for every malady, but we need to keep the wineskins of our mind elastic enough to receive new ideas.

Here's the prevailing chemical theory about depression: When we don't have enough serotonin (a neurotransmitter that acts as a feel-good hormone) in our system because it is absorbed too quickly or in too great a quantity by the neurons in our brain, then depression is likely to occur.

Maybe it would be helpful to think about it like baseball.

When you have two cells, one acting as the pitcher and the other as the catcher, if the pitcher just tosses the ball in the air and catches it himself, that is like reabsorbing the serotonin. When this happens, then the catcher won't be able to catch it (the good mood that serotonin produces). Popular antidepressants are known as selective serotonin reuptake inhibitors (SSRIs). They work by blocking the pitcher's ability to keep the ball to himself, and they send the good vibes winging their way to the catcher. When a problem occurs in how the brain is working with serotonin, this is the only way to hit the home run of feeling better.

Between any two neurotransmitters in our brain is a space we call a synapse. For the presynaptic neuron to stop latching on to the sero-tonin too rapidly after pitching it to the postsynaptic neuron, SSRIs can slow the reabsorption. When depression is caused by the serotonin being absorbed too quickly or in too great of a quantity, the SSRI can save the day.

Despite loads of testimonies showcasing the effectiveness of these med-ications, some Christians view them as taboo. Which only goes to show how religious thinking can sometimes lag behind where innovation offers to take us.

Forward progress is always hampered by a closed mind. We love our prejudices and are sometimes stuck in old ways of thinking. When they were first introduced, nearly every great invention was treated with sus-picion—trains, automobiles, planes, and computers were all suspect and thought to be too dangerous to embrace. When Jonas Hanway first introduced the umbrella into the UK, he had to weather a storm of insults as he walked down the street with it open above his head.[3]

Religious mindsets are often notorious for shutting down progress. Think of how the Catholic church made Copernicus retract his state-ment that the earth revolved around the sun, not vice versa. Church leaders were convinced that the earth was the center of the solar system, so they couldn't abide Copernicus's newfangled ideas.

When new medicines have been introduced, there has often been a storm of controversy. Sir James Simpson pioneered the use of chloro-form as an anesthetic to save the world from pain. There has probably been no greater discovery for the alleviation of unnecessary agony, but at first many religious people were opposed to it. They believed that pain could purify the soul, so they didn't think it was right to relieve it through anesthesia.[4]

All this should bring to mind the words of Jesus: "No one sews a patch of unshrunk cloth on an old garment, for the patch will pull away from the garment, making the tear worse. Neither do men pour new wine into old wineskins. If they do, the skins will burst, the wine will run out and the wineskins will be ruined. No, they pour new wine into new wineskins, and both are preserved" (Matthew 9:16-17).

I think one of the things Jesus is getting at here is the necessity of adaptability. If we can't adjust and move ahead along a new path, we might become stuck in the past. A lot of our attitudes in the area of medication and counseling are a matter of loving our old wineskins so much that we aren't open to the new gifts of God that come through medicine and psychology.

We are long overdue for removing the stigma from antidepressants.

((((( )))))

Let's work to change attitudes about depression, counseling, and medication so that people can get the help they need.

We should use all the tools God has given us to get better. We are integrated beings, with body, soul, and spirit all rolled into one. We can make use of the medicines in the pharmacy as well as homeopathic cures. We can get ourselves healthy by clean eating and bodyweight exercises. We can get counseling, and we can pray for healing. Sometimes when we pray for healing, God will answer through doctors and medicine. The eyes of El Roi sometimes look at us through the eyes of our physician. Remember, Luke, the author of one of the Gospels, was a doctor...and he was a man who recorded great miracles of healing.[5]

((((( )))))

Some forms of psychology are overly concerned with clever theories that explain all our problems. So many different ideas are out there, and a psychological convention can sometimes look like the intellectual equivalent of an NHL free-for-all brawl. Psychologists offer their competing constructs to help us understand our behaviors. That's why they pose binaries like *introvert* and *extrovert*, assign colors or numbers to our personalities, ask us to analyze our dreams for deeper meanings, try to expose the psychological scar tissue that arises from the way we were raised, or grapple with the difference between our conscious and unconscious responses. These are all concepts that might help us better understand ourselves and why we do what we do.

Or…

They might just be the fruit of creative thinking. All these ideas (and many more) are theories that might be true…or might not be true. The whole history of psychology is a history of theories put forward with passion and certainty, only to be withdrawn as a "better" explanation replaces them.

Which is why I believe the best counseling is based upon brain science.

Neuroscience is a different animal from speculative psychology. It focuses on observable facts rather than abstract theories. And it might just be a better guide to our psychological well-being and happiness.

Neuroscience is based upon the evidence of brain scans. It can show you what is going on in your brain. It isn't about creating a grand story that explains your odd quirks and the problems you struggle with. It's about looking into what the facts are telling us.

For example, neuroscience tells us that what we practice is what we become. That what we do makes us who we are. Now, you might not feel that you are one of those hopeful people who can always see a positive future, but you can build muscle memory in your brain in that direction by acting and speaking as though you were feeling hope. And then, eventually, you'll find that you are settling into a sunnier worldview. This more joyful way of thinking about life becomes instinctive!

We become who we want to become. Our habits make us who we are.

There is such hope in this point of view. You might be predisposed toward depression, but you are most certainly not doomed to *being* a depressed person. You do not have to be stuck on a treadmill of pain and ennui. You can feel better. "Neuroplasticity" is the technical word for the phenomenon of how our brain can be remolded into whatever shape we desire it to be. Through rote and repetitious thinking, you can literally rewire the neural pathways in your brain in order to jolt them out of unhealthy grooves. If your thoughts run toward the dark, you can reorient them toward the light. Your attitude can become healthy again by thinking about hopeful ideas and ideals—over and over again.

Maybe something like this was what Paul had in mind when he wrote of taking our thoughts captive. Neuroplasticity shows that our brain is plastic, elastic, and malleable; and through practice we can reshape it! The psychiatrist Daniel Amen has performed more brain scans than anyone in history. After 22 years and 83,000 brain scans, the single most important lesson he and his colleagues have discovered is that the brain *can* change.[6]

How we think affects how we feel, so maybe it's time to readjust our thinking. And that begins with taking a happier outlook. It might be difficult at first. You may feel like you're faking it. But in the end, your whole take on life can be transformed.

We can go beyond all the wild and wonderful concepts of psychology theory and embrace real change through neuroplasticity. Your brain's chemistry is not static but kinetic.

In the words of neurobiologist Carla Shatz, "What fires together, wires together." (Now that's a bumper sticker I might actually affix to my car…)

To use an analogy from the world of vinyl records, you can literally escape the grooves of doom and gloom that just keep taking you around and around, meaninglessly circling the abyss. You can find a better groove in which to groove. You don't have to live in a dark, unconscious netherworld where strange things swim. You are not the product of your parents' psychosis. The prophet Ezekiel said children shouldn't say their teeth were set on edge because their fathers ate sour grapes—which was a proverbial way of saying, "Don't blame your parents for the way you are" (Ezekiel 18:2-3). Nor are you "just made that way." You are not locked into being an introvert or an extrovert or a number on the Enneagram. You are not stuck.

It's time to get the help you need.

It's time to jump the groove!

WEAPON #10:
LET GOD LOVE ON YOU

Did you know the words "radical" and "radish" have the same origin? They both come from the Latin word *radix*, which means "root." A radish is a root plant, and radical means going to the root. In this chapter I'd like to invite you to go to your roots, namely the fact that God radically loves you. We've already looked at a whole bunch of things that can help you defeat depression—nine weapons that have proven indispensable to me, and which I believe can benefit you. They are all useful, but the one I want to share with you now is the most important one of all, the one that makes the greatest difference in how you perceive your life and your world…

Let God love on you.

In other words, you don't need to do anything but just sit there and let God love the heavens right into you and the despair clean out of you.

((((( )))))

When I talk about God, I know that the very mention of His name carries a lot of baggage for some people. They hear the word "God" and immediately think about those people who claim to be His followers and deny the value of science or oppress women. Can I just remind you that these things are not the result of God but the result of religion? God invented science. Hey, science is, in a sense, just a collection of footnotes for His act of creation. When it comes to women, Jesus was someone who was ahead of His time in His attitudes toward them. In the Jewish culture at that time, a Samaritan woman was seen as having less value than a donkey, and a man who had a prolonged conversation with a woman in public was in danger of the fires of hell. But Jesus's longest recorded one-on-one conversation was with a Samaritan woman! He treated women with honor and respect in a culture that generally didn't. The Bible never says the disciples were amazed when Jesus walked on water or fed the five thousand with a lunch box, but it does say they were amazed when He spoke with a woman! (John 4:27 NASB).

Jesus wasn't pro-religion. In fact, it was religion that put Him on the cross. He didn't come to form a religious institution; He came to set people free. I think if Jesus found out that we'd started a religion in His name, He would probably shake His head and say, "You did what?"

So, when I start talking about God, you can be assured that what I'm offering is spirituality without all the religious baggage—the love of God without the rules of man. Honestly, I'm not that interested in talking about the religion of Christianity. I just want to introduce you to a penniless teacher from Nazareth who would go on a mission to the ends of the earth, even to a cross, to prove that His Father loves you to death, and that His lovingkindness is better than life.

((((( )))))

The apostle John defined God in the simplest terms: "God is love" (1 John 4:8). Jesus, whose every action seemed rooted in love, told His disciples that "anyone who has seen me has seen the Father" (John 14:9). He was, according to Paul, "the image of the invisible God" (Colossians

1:15). That word "image" is the Greek word *eikon*, a word that referred to an accurate portrait of someone. When we see Jesus, therefore, we understand what God looks like. He reveals that the mystery of God is revealed in the person of Jesus Christ, and that Jesus is all about love. So, therefore, is God the Father.

People are groping in the dark trying to find God.

- Is He a Goody Two-shoes, moralistic judge, as some fundamentalist Christians seem to believe?

- Is He an impersonal cosmic force and not really a person at all, as many Buddhists teach?

- Is He the divine spark in every living thing, as the Hindus assert?

- Is He a non-relational warrior, as certain factions of Islam teach?

- Is He a figment of the imagination and a comforting delusion for the weak minded, as atheists proclaim?

How do we know what is true?

We look at Jesus, the very image of a God of love. He didn't come to help us pick the right religion. Jesus showed us a God who would hang naked on a cross to show us just how crazy He is about you and me.

In my life, time and again, God has reminded me of His love. I remember a day when my friends and I visited a valley filled with beautiful waterfalls. The treetops were reflected in their pools, and the rapids were whiter than moonlight on snow. The dell smelled of moss and springtime. Cameron and I ventured out onto a giant rock in the middle of the river, and we dangled our feet above the surface of the rushing water. The day was slipping away, and it seemed as though it had run out of things to say. A hush fell over everything around us, and we sat there quietly as the sunset flamed out and nightfall arrived. The stars sparkled above us.

We just sat in silence.

This was a year after my life had seemed to fall apart, and there was nothing more left to say about it. We just sat there quietly on that rock in the middle of the river, and let God love on us.

Soon I felt God's affection sweep over me like the water over the rocks. At that moment I felt no fear and no regrets. I asked no questions. I just let God love on me.

I felt that He not only loved me, but that He *adored* me. It was an experience I'll never forget, and a reality I have felt many times since then.

((((( )))))

What do *you* believe about God?

This isn't an abstract question. Researchers have found that what you believe about God not only affects your emotional health but is also a huge component of identity formation. It makes a difference in how your brain functions. It is at the very core of who you are. It affects how you think about yourself, as well as how you relate to others. How you perceive God dictates what you receive from Him.

A.W. Tozer said, "What I believe about God is the most important thing about me." That is so true. What you believe about God will influence everything about the way you think as well as how you live your life.

You'll never feel better about your life or about yourself unless you have the right perspective about God.

Which is why it's absolutely critical that you understand the truth about who God really is and how He feels about you.

The truth: God adores you, and anything you've heard that contradicts that is a lie.

(((( ))))

You've probably heard of the "Four Spiritual Laws." Well, I think we need to understand the "Four Spiritual *Lies*," the mistakes we commonly make in our understanding of God:

1. God is angry at you. He is basically a ticked-off Landlord, mad at His tenants on planet Earth for messing this place up.

2. God will remain angry at you unless you become religious.

3. God wants you to be burdened with a whole laundry list of rules.

4. If you follow all the rules, then, and only then, will God tolerate you.

(((( ))))

On the other hand, there is one great truth about God:

1. God is love.

That's it. Period. End of story.

There is no alternative truth about the nature of things. There are no ifs, ands, or buts; no exceptions or annexations or stipulations; no opt-out clauses. And there sure as heaven isn't any bad news to balance out the good news.

God loves you. That is all. No strings attached. Those goofy signs people hold up at sporting events that say "John 3:16" actually point to something true. If you look that up in the Bible, you'll see that God so loved the world that He gave His Son. This is a truth that seems worthy of a little celebration in the end zone.

What this means is that the chief forces of the universe are on your side. God, the Principle Behind Which You Cannot Go, the Ultimate Reality, the Ground of Being, the Source, the Architect, and the Author of All Our Stories—He is *for* you. This universe isn't an indifferent, inimical, or hostile place. It's a place where your journey is being written by the Creator. An epic worthy of Milton and a love story more compelling than Shakespeare.

So, let Him love on you.

And remember that this isn't just a story about your existence right now. It's more like a fairy tale. You *can* live happily ever after. This life? Well, it's just the prologue to that never-ending story.

There is a reason why almost all people throughout time have believed in an afterlife. It isn't just wishful thinking. It is baked into our DNA. God has "set eternity in the human heart" (Ecclesiastes 3:11). An inextinguishable spark in each of us has been fashioned for eternity. Nothing can snuff that out.

God's love is the most powerful force in the universe.

May *that* force be with you.

(((( ))))

Do you believe God personifies and embodies love? I hope so, because that belief is integral to everything. It's the basis for all healthy thinking.

When you pray to the God who is Love, it has the effect of decluttering your thinking. It provides focus and clarity and helps you see things as they really are. It helps you be more loving and forgiving toward others. And it gives you a clearer picture about who you are. A lot of people feel depressed because they feel that no one understands them, that they are alone, that they are a misfit.

The good news is that you are not alone, and that God loves misfits just like you!

(((( ))))

When Buddhist monks talk about what they call "the monkey mind," they are referring to an experience most of us know all too well. We find it hard to focus on what is right in front of us because our brain jumps from topic to topic the way a monkey swings from branch to branch as it travels from tree to tree. This way of thinking doesn't get us very far. It just creates confusion and a total lack of focus.

The best cure for the monkey mind—the most effective tool for helping us think clearly and correctly about our lives—is to experience the focus that comes from praying to the God who loves us. So, if you feel like your thoughts run off with every squirrel—if your mind wanders and seldom comes back—there is something you can do. When you are feeling a little ADHD or ADD or just plain SAD, you can open your heart to the One who cherishes you, and His love will soothe your spirit.

(((( ))))

Sometimes people ask me, "How can I get closer to God?"

My reply is simple: You really can't. How can you get any closer to a God who already lives inside you? A God who makes His presence known within your heart and mind? He has made a home within you. How much closer can you get?

He doesn't make it difficult for us. Jesus said that His burden is light (Matthew 11:30), so if your walk with God seems difficult and heavy, it's because you are doing it wrong!

Just let God love on you.

He has already taken the initiative.

He has already given you an invitation.

Now just sit back, bask in the Presence, and let God give you a sloppy bear hug!

WEAPON #11: DREAMALITY

It's easy to get stuck in a rut when it comes to how we are thinking about our life.

Many people never stop and look at their life from a different angle. Instead, they just keep on plugging away in the same direction, even when it seems as though they are going nowhere.

We need to give more energy to chasing our dreams than worrying about our nightmares. We have approximately 50,000 thoughts a day,[1] so when's the last time you stopped to think about what you were thinking about?

Warren Wiersbe wrote, "Outlook determines outcome." So if your out-look gets bleak, then try the uplook! When you change the way you look at things, things start to change the way they look. Because the problem is never just the problem but your perception about the problem. And when you think your problem is too big for you, then it's just the right size for God. And your prayers will be a problem for your problems!

(((((( ))))))

What we need to do if we want to make changes in our lives is to get a fresh perspective. We need to have the guts to take everything we think we know and turn it upside down.

To read the first page of this chapter, you had to turn this book upside down and break out of the way you've been reading it. You might just need to do the same thing with your life. Stop and take a fresh look. See it from a new point of view.

What needs to be changed?

How might you think differently about the things you are struggling with?

How can you take that next holistic step you need to make?

Sometimes the road out of depression starts with having the courage to look at your life from a viewpoint you've never considered before.

It's never too late to turn your life on its head!

You'll never climb out of your depression and stay out of it unless you change the thinking that got you there—and might well be keeping you there.

Too much of our thinking is about defending ourselves from pain rather than chasing our dreams. If you want to get out of the cycle of depression, you need to start thinking like a winner.

After all, the Bible says that 1) death is swallowed up in victory because 2) the battle is the Lord's and 3) He is a warrior who 4) never loses, which means 5) if God be for us, who can stand against us? So, it's no wonder that 6) no weapon formed against us shall prosper.[2]

(I like spiritual warfare because I like winning.)

Mic drop.

((((( )))))

Forget about taking a defensive and protective posture toward life. Jesus said the gates of Hades won't prevail against us (Matthew 16:18). Keep in mind that gates are not offensive weapons but defensive mechanisms. We don't attack someone by throwing a gate at them. Gates are part of the enemy's defense. When I'm going through a spiritual attack, it's because I am the one who is attacking!

Life isn't about putting out fires. It's about starting them.

Life isn't about trying as hard as we can to keep from doing the wrong thing. It's about realizing that all we can do is win. Which, of course, begs the question: What would you do with your life if you knew you couldn't fail?

((((( )))))

You are already in the winner's circle. Don't believe any different.

Jesus said on the cross that "it is finished" (John 19:30). He meant that with His sacrifice, all the work has been done. The cross is the coup de grace, a "finish 'em off" move, a "game over" for the enemy, and the incontrovertible evidence of God's love. Anything extra is just for fun— cherries on top of the cake, extra credit, and bonus rounds.

Letting you follow your dreams has always been on God's agenda for you.

- Psalm 20:4: "May he [the Lord] give you the desire of your heart."

- Psalm 21:2: "You [God] have granted him his heart's desire."

- Psalm 37:4: "Take delight in the Lord, and he will give you the desires of your heart."

- Psalm 145:19: "He fulfills the desires of those who fear him."

- Proverbs 10:24: "What the righteous desire will be granted."

- Proverbs 13:12: "Hope deferred makes the heart sick, but when the desire comes, it is a tree of life" (NKJV).

When you walk with, talk to, follow after, trust in, lean into, and depend upon the God of hope, His plans and your dreams sync up like the Bluetooth that pairs with your devices. He loves to give you your heart's desires…because He implanted them in your heart in the first place.

((((( )))))

Let me ask you again: What would you do with your life if you knew you couldn't fail?

Because failing is not in your stars. Victory is your birthright.

Sure, there will be setbacks here and there along the journey, but the destination is set, and it shimmers out there in the near distance. Keep chasing it. It's within reach.

We've got to stop playing scared. We've got to stop playing with a focus on *not* losing. We can wholeheartedly go after the win.

All too many Christians look like they were baptized in lemon juice. We don't have to take that approach because—spoiler alert—the enemy *will* lose and we *will* win! As Mark Batterson said, "Jesus didn't die to keep us safe. He died to make us dangerous." He founded an army of resistance fighters to battle against the forces of darkness and hopelessness and despair. And you and I have been invited to join His battalion. He's looking for volunteers who aren't about living safely but about living victoriously.

One of the reasons I couldn't break free from my state of depression for so long was because I was dedicated to playing it safe. I let the whole religious system swallow my identity, and I didn't dare to dream my dreams. I tried to be vanilla, to blend in, to not rock the boat. Moving away from my heart got me nowhere in a hurry because all the while God was quietly wooing me to go more deeply *into* my heart. As Lou Engle notes, when God made me, He created a dream and wrapped a body around it…and He did the same for you.

(((( )))))

What are we if not the sum of our dreams?

When I finally decided to pursue my heart's desires again, I found hope. And one by one, my impossible dreams became realities.

So, dream bravely, my friends.

Don't listen to what the grownups said so often. You *should* get your hopes up!

Lawrence of Arabia wrote: "All men dream: but not equally. Those who dream by night in the dusty recesses of their minds wake in the day to find that it was vanity: but the dreamers of the day are dangerous men, for they may act on their dreams with open eyes, to make it possible."[3] Yep.

Our dreams are connected to God's promises. He promises to fulfill the desires of our heart. (The real ones, though, not the twisted and selfish ones birthed by our narcissistic culture). It might take 25 years, as it did for Abraham, who was awaiting a son. Or 13 years, as it did for Joseph, who rose from the bottom of a pit to become a man of power and influence. Or 15 years, as it did for David, who waited a long time between his anointing and his rise to the throne.

There is a good reason why the Bible says "wait on the Lord" no less than 106 times.

In the end, God is always faithful about keeping His word.

As my sister Mary texted me the other day, "I'm still here because I will not let a nightmare have more power than my dreams."

Well said.

You can keep on believing.

That is the best way you can begin to defeat depression.

PART THREE

DANCING

IN THE

LIGHT

OF TOLKIEN, LEWIS, AND THE PHRYGIAN LEGEND

I imagine virtually everyone knows the story of Frodo Baggins and his companions on their epic quest to defeat evil. If you haven't read *The Lord of the Rings* series, you've likely seen the movie. But most people don't know the story of the man who created Middle Earth, J.R.R. Tolkien.

Tolkien fought in the trenches of World War I and experienced all the horrors of that war. Though a reluctant soldier, he joined the army out of a sense of duty. He survived the battle of the Somme, where so many of his dearest friends and fellow soldiers were killed, but it left a mark on his psyche. What he suffered as a result was traumatic shock, survivor's guilt, and a deep sense of loss. What he had seen was a horror almost beyond description.

It took many years for Tolkien to fully process what he had gone through, and when he did, he channeled these experiences into fiction as he composed his great trilogy. The world he created mirrored the trauma of fiercest battle. As he penned the books, he was able to reflect upon the meaning of such things as war, human nature, loss, and the purpose of life. He shaped his trauma into an unforgettable story that still touches readers at every level. As we read it today, joining Aragorn and the Hobbits on their quest to defeat the dark lord Sauron and his minions, their trials and tribulations can help us better cope with our own struggles and wounds. As we revel in the beauty of Tolkien's masterful storytelling, our emotions are stirred into taking up arms against the things that oppress our psyches.

Tolkien reclaimed his own life through the stories he told. And reading them has helped me reclaim my own life.

He told a tale that arose out of his own PTSD and thereby demonstrated that post-traumatic growth is something we can all reach for. Tolkien went on to become one of the world's foremost philologists and a professor at Oxford. His success inspires me to believe that my own PTSD can be redeemed. It might even be a foundation from which I can change the world!

((((( )))))

One of Tolkien's best friends was Oxford don C.S. Lewis. He was the author of the classic *Chronicles of Narnia* and several dozen other amazing books. Lewis was wounded and hospitalized during that same global conflict. An article titled "War Made C.S. Lewis" tells us this,

> Creeping forward with his company was 2nd Lt. Clive Staples Lewis, an Irishman who could have avoided serving in the British Army but who never even considered sitting out the war.
>
> A shell exploded—whether it was German or British is a matter of debate—instantly killing a nearby sergeant and peppering Lewis with shrapnel. He was severely wounded when the metal shards lodged in his left wrist, left leg and upper left ribs, the third piece puncturing his left lung.
>
> "Just after I was hit, I found (or thought I found) that I was not breathing and concluded that this was death," Lewis later wrote.

"I felt no fear and certainly no courage. It did not seem to be an occasion for either."

The Lewis who crawled away from the carnage was not yet the C.S. Lewis of *The Chronicles of Narnia, The Space Trilogy, The Screwtape Letters* and *Mere Christianity*. Then, he was like so many others who fought in World War I—just another wounded soldier desperate not to bleed to death.[1]

Lewis would go on to become one of the most accomplished defenders of the Christian faith and a celebrated scholar of Medieval and Renaissance literature. Like Tolkien, he considered his experience in the Great War to be one of the most influential events in his life.

((((( )))))

Whereas Tolkien simply channeled his thoughts about war into his great novels, Lewis directly addressed what he had experienced. He does not glamorize what he went through:

I have gone to sleep marching and woken again and found myself marching still…The frights, the cold, the smell of H.E., the horribly smashed men still moving like half-crushed beetles, the sitting or standing corpses, the landscape of sheer earth without a blade of grass, the boots worn day and night till they seemed to grow to your feet—all this shows rarely and faintly in memory. It is too cut off from the rest of my experience and often seems to have happened to someone else…This is War. This is what Homer wrote about.[2]

But he made it through. He survived and went on to have a life that has impacted millions of people. The mark of the conflict was indelible, but he emerged stronger for it.

((((( )))))

Lewis and Tolkien demonstrate the incredible resilience of human beings. They show that we can bounce back from even the harshest traumas, and maybe even create something great as a result, like the writings these two literary giants produced.

Maybe our battles with depression can have a similar result.

What if the wounds from our conflicts and spiritual warfare are the weapons the Captain of our Salvation uses to unleash a defeat upon the enemy of our soul?

((((( )))))

The ancient Phrygians had a legend that each time they conquered an enemy, the victor *absorbed* the physical strength of his victim and added that much more to his own valor and strength.

Could it be that when we nobly face our own warfare that our spiritual life force is doubled?

In the Bible, the prophet Isaiah speaks of "flying on the shoulders" of Israel's hated opponent, the Philistines (Isaiah 11:14 KJV). These deadly foes, he seems to be suggesting, would not only be defeated but would carry the Israelites on their backs to even greater victories. Depression is not only a foe we must defeat, but it may also be the shoulders on which we are carried to further triumphs.

((((( )))))

The battle against depression requires the spirit of a warrior. We who struggle against a foe as fearsome as Despair know that the battle will often be brutal and bloody, but we know we can overcome our enemy. The Bible is honest about how hard life can be. If you removed all the stories about struggling people, doubters, the afflicted, the grieving, and the sorrowful from its pages, you'd have a much smaller book. The Bible is unflinching about telling these non-flattering tales. Plenty of violence and bloodshed are in its pages. Plenty of guts and gore. Perhaps it's preparing us for life as it must be lived in this fallen world.

(((( )))))

God doesn't shrink back when your life feels like a war movie!

Jesus was born into a war. A war for the Kingdom of God.

Paul said he was crucified with Christ so that he no longer lived—but Christ lived in him (Galatians 2:20).

We cannot experience the resurrection if we haven't experienced the cross. You can't ride on the shoulders of Philistines unless they have been defeated. You cannot draw the life force from the enemy unless you face him in battle.

Depression can be a bloody affair. It can feel as if it's going to kill you… or make you want to kill yourself. But Tolkien and Lewis offer prime examples of how you can take all the battle weariness and woundedness you've experienced and turn them into fuel for changing your life and changing your world. You'll never write your own *The Last Battle* or *The Return of the King* until you've experienced the Great War yourself.

We have one greater than Aragorn who fights at our side.

We are the children of Aslan.

THEOLOGY
AND THIEF-OLOGY

If you want to make a difference in your own life, and in the world, you need to become someone who isn't satisfied with the way things are. You need to stop being a follower and become a leader.

What is a leader? Someone who seeks to raze the conformist culture to the ground and raise earth to heaven. Someone who is like the great painters of the Renaissance, who ignored the boxes into which the church and the culture tried to place them and instead splashed their creativity across their canvases and across the canvas of culture. They were an alarm clock for the soul of those who saw, through their work, a whole new way of looking at the world. That is what a leader does, whether it be with their paintbrush, their words, or their courageous actions.

The passion of a real leader is to thumb his or her nose at mediocrity. It reflects the passion of a God who has never settled for doing things in an average and halfhearted way.

God wants to jolt our thoughts and aspirations out of the settled groves of the mundane and send them spinning into fantastical and hopeful places.

Let's face it. God is magical.

And our faith should be too.

((((( )))))

We celebrate the God who exploded the solar systems into existence.

It's a big place.

The Milky Way contains 100 billion stars,[1] and there are 800,000 cataloged insects that crawl on the earth.[2]

Psalm 8 tells us that God fashioned the stars with His fingers. He made the gaseous nebulae collapse into stars, set all the planets into orbit, and populated at least one of them with an overwhelming variety of critters. You are one of them.

Think what a God that big is capable of doing in your life…

He wants so much more for you than the mediocrity that is usually on our culture's menu. He has an almost unimaginable desire to see you find your best path. He is relentless in His pursuit of your heart and mind.

When David wrote that goodness and mercy would follow him all the days of his life, the Hebrew word behind "follow" is *radaph*. It's a word often used to describe the actions of Israel's aggressive foes. *Radaph* can actually be translated as "to hunt."[3] How epic! God's goodness and mercy literally HUNT us down!

I love the thought that I am being hunted by goodness and mercy.

((((( )))))

God is not mad at you. He is madly in love with you.

He loves to send good things to chase you down. If your view of God is that He is seeking to kill and steal and destroy your dreams, think again. This isn't theology, it is "thief-ology" (see John 10:10). So, readjust your perceptions. Take His love seriously.

The right kind of theology makes all the difference in how you think about your life. It will not pull you down into guilt and despair but instead lift you up into a life of adventure and passion and hope.

Don't lower your theology down to match your reality.

Raise your reality up to your theology!

As the saying goes, "Don't downgrade your dreams to match your reality. Upgrade your faith to match your vision."

BRAIN POWER!

Consider for a moment the humble human brain, weighing on average about three pounds, and normally the size of two large fists. Frankly, it looks like something that was left out in the rain a little too long, all wrinkled and slightly misshapen.

But the human brain is the most complicated arrangement of matter in the universe.

It has between 86 to 100 billion neurons.[1]

Even though it cannot move from its place in your noggin, it consumes up to 20 percent of your nutrients and oxygen.[2] It's an energy hog, but it more than earns its keep.

After all the study and research, our brains are still something of a mystery. We really only understand about 2-8 percent of how it works. What we do understand, though, is nothing short of astonishing. Scientists believe that our brains can store roughly a million gigabytes of information.[3] That means you have an enormous library right there between your ears.

Are you making good use of it?

Let's review some activities which are beneficial for our brains, because don't we really want to use ours for all it's worth?

First, reading. There is a good reason an old slogan exists—readers are leaders. You'll be hard pressed to find an effective leader who doesn't love books. Maybe it's time to ask yourself what's on your nightstand. Have you read a good book lately?

Second, exercise. Go ahead and sigh, but you know it's true. You need to work your body to keep your brain working at its best. Remember, a 40-minute jog has the same effect on your brain as a strong antidepressant…and without any negative side effects. So, is it time to get up off the couch?

Third, praying and meditating. Research shows that when people talk with God the frontal lobe of their brain fires up into the highest intellectual state.[4] In other words, you actually become smarter by praying! But it matters who these prayers are addressed to. If you pray to an angry God, it increases the activity in your amygdala, and you are more easily angered and less tolerant of others. You will probably also become more stressed. But if you pray to a God of love and acceptance, you develop a richer and thicker gray matter in your prefrontal cortex (responsible for rational decision-making) and your anterior cingulate cortex (associated with warm and fuzzy feelings) will be engaged.

People who believe in a loving God develop stronger focus and more compassion and have lower stress levels and lower blood pressure. They also find it easier to forgive others and let their resentment go. In other words, they are more likely to act like Jesus.

Such people also tend to laugh more. Psalm 37 tells us that God laughs, and when you laugh like your Creator, you are actually boosting your brain power.

So here is my prescription for your cranial package: Crack open a book, go for a walk or a jog, talk to the Lord of Love, and have a good laugh. Your brain will thank you for it.

BULLETPROOF SOULS

John, the writer of the fourth Gospel, penned these words in his letter to fellow Christians: "This is love: not that we loved God, but that he loved us" (1 John 4:10). Maybe that's why John was one of the few who stood by Jesus when He was hung on a cross.

Peter didn't.

Perhaps Peter was too focused on what he perceived as the strength of his faith; too reliant on how much he was committed to Jesus to actually come through in the pinch. "Even if I have to die with you, I will never disown you," he said with bravado (Matthew 26:35). His passionate declaration sounded heroic, but words alone didn't cut it when the time came for courage and for love in action.

John called himself "the one Jesus loved" in his Gospel (John 20:2), but he never identified himself as that beloved person. He wasn't trying to say that he was Jesus's favorite. He was just in awe of how much Jesus loved him. I believe it was that recognition of Jesus's love that gave him the courage to stand by as He was crucified.

Peter, on the other hand, was focused upon *his* love for Jesus; that he was a disciple who loved Jesus. When the moment of truth came, he ended up denying that he even knew Him.

John was focused on *Jesus's* love for him; that he was a disciple whom Jesus loved—and he took his place at the foot of the cross. John, who had leaned on his Lord's breast, had the courage to march to the beat of Christ's heart. Peter saw himself as the disciple who loved Jesus, which is why he forsook the Lord. John saw himself as the disciple whom Jesus loved, which is why he never left his Lord's side.

((((( )))))

So, when you are thinking about the love of God, remember it's not primarily about you. It's about Him; about His fierce and unrelenting love for you, not about how much religious commitment you can muster for Him.

The Song of Songs insists that "many waters cannot quench love" (8:7). Love is unquenchable and immortal. When you think about it, there is really no practical social utility in loving people who have already died, but we do. We love our deceased family and friends now—in the present—not just in the past tense.

History tells us that apostle whom Jesus loved was poisoned by the authorities as punishment for his love of Jesus, but he did not die. Then he was burned in a cauldron of boiling oil and still didn't die. Finally, he was abandoned on a desert island. But instead of dying, he had a vision of God's ultimate triumph and wrote a book about it—the Revelation of John.

Not only did he not die, but he came back with a bestseller!

((((( )))))

Once, while Teddy Roosevelt was giving a public address, an assassin shot him. But his long-windedness saved his life. His copious notes for the speech, along with his eyeglass case, provided makeshift armor and prevented fatal damage. With the bullet lodged in his body, he still managed to finish presenting his speech!

Like Roosevelt, we cannot be stopped.

We have bulletproof souls.

THE CHAPTER
THAT STARTS WITH
A LOUSY JOKE

Twenty years ago, we had Johnny Cash, Bob Hope, and Steve Jobs.

Then they died.

Now we have no cash, no hope, and no jobs.

Please, God, don't let Kevin Bacon die.

((((( )))))

That's from Bill Murray, and it effectively captures the reality of what it feels like to be part of my generation in these troubled times. No cash, no hope, no jobs is the situation that many of us struggle with every day. It can sometimes be a tough time to be alive. In 2017, suicide was the second leading cause of death in the US for people aged 10-34.[1]

If our generation is feeling so hopeless, then what is our first step out of that dark tunnel?

Are you ready for my profound response?

We need to have more fun. Fun is fundamental.

Frankly, life seems a lot better when you take a whole lot of things a whole lot less seriously. The Bible tells us that we can have "joy unspeakable" (1 Peter 1:8 KJV). If we can't fully speak of this joy, then perhaps we can show it by the way we live our lives. We can be nonconformists, joyous rebels, and professional fun-havers. We can say no to our despair and depression, and yes to a different way of looking at our lives.

That doesn't mean all our problems will vanish in a puff of smoke, but it does mean that we never need to be hopeless when we are going through our worst because God is planning His best for us.

((((( )))))

Mary and Joseph held tight to Jesus when they went down into Egypt to escape Herod's soldiers, who were seeking to kill the child. Egypt had once been the land where the Hebrews suffered in bondage for 400 years.

Eight years later Mary and Joseph lost their 12-year-old son in the crowds in Jerusalem during Passover, the time when Jews celebrated their deliverance from Egypt. They panicked when they couldn't find Him. Perhaps God allowed Jesus's parents to suffer this feverish perplexity to cure them of the lethargy that comes with security.

There is another ancient story that when little baby Jesus was taken to Egypt, all the idols fell down in His presence. A powerful toddler, indeed. Jesus, the image of the invisible God, has the power to destroy the idols in our lives, and He can teach us how to lean into God's strength in the midst of our adversities.

It's easier to lose sight of the Christ dimension in your life during seasons of celebration. We tend to lose track of the Lord during festivity, and we tend to keep Him close during adversity. But it's in these happy seasons that we need to cling more tightly to the Lord's hand.

The time of being trapped in our depression is behind us. The day of the optimisfits has come!

THE THANKSLIVING
GRATITUDE ATTITUDE

Thanksgiving is not just a holiday, an opportunity for a long weekend.

Thanksgiving should be our lifestyle.

When Jesus healed ten lepers, only one of them turned back to offer thanks to Him (Luke 17:11-19). The others just went on their way—happy but oblivious. Let's decide that we will approach our life like the guy who took the time to stop and say, "Thank you."

According to a scientific study, people who are more grateful are more likely to give money to good causes. They want to spread the happiness of a gratitude attitude. This same study found that these people also showed greater neural sensitivity in the medial prefrontal cortex of their brain, the area associated with learning and decision making.[1] Grateful people, in other words, show more wisdom in their words and actions.

The Bible states the goal pretty clearly: "Give thanks in all circumstances" (1 Thessalonians 5:18).

The prophet Malachi says that when we speak words which honor God's name, He "hearkens" and writes our conversations down in a book of remembrance (Malachi 3:16 KJV). The Hebrew word translated "hearken" is the same word used to describe a dog's ears perking up when it hears something that interests him.

It takes 72 different muscles to produce speech.

On average, most people speak about 16,000 words every day. How many of your words causes God's ears to perk up?

Out of the 860.3 million words you'll speak in your lifetime,[2] how many of them will be words of thankfulness?

24

THE INEFFABLE
TETRAGRAMMATON

In the Old Testament, the ineffable, unspeakable name of God was called the *Tetragrammaton*.

It was spelled YHWH because in the written Hebrew language there are no vowels, only consonants. Interestingly, YHWH are the only consonants that cannot be spoken with the tongue or with the lips closed. Go ahead and try.

Why?

Because the pronunciation of the sacred name of God was an attempt to replicate the act of breathing. The ancient rabbis taught that to correctly say the name of God, you basically inhale "Yah," and exhale "Weh." So, every breath was, in a sense, a declaration of His name.

As Rob Bell has noted, the first thing you "said" when you emerged from your mother's womb was the name of God.

And "God" is the last thing you say when you die.

One might even say that you don't die when you stop breathing.

You die when you can no longer say the name of God…

So, when an atheist confidently states that there is no God—even as these words emerge from their mouth, they are breathing His name without realizing it.[1]

And when Paul encourages believers to "pray without ceasing" (1 Thessalonians 5:17 KJV), they are, in a sense, doing exactly that with every breath.

Which is why the word "spirit" and the word "breath" are the same in virtually every major language. The spirit is as near as your next breath.

Before He returned to heaven, Jesus breathed on the gathered disciples and imparted the Spirit to them (John 20:22). God created Adam, according to Genesis, by breathing into the dust and the dust became a living being (Genesis 2:7).

Paul wrote that "godliness with contentment is great gain" (1 Timothy 6:6). The word picture in the original Greek is meant to conjure the image of a little baby resting in the lap of its daddy and letting out a contented sigh. So, as a child of Abba, you can rest in His everlasting arms, breathing prayers in the Spirit with groanings that cannot be uttered (Romans 8:26 KJV).

When life feels overly challenging, maybe it's time to take a deep breath.

Asking the question, "Where is God?" when your heart is hurting is like asking, "What shape is yellow?"

Truth is, God is as near to you as your next breath.

25

BRIEFCASES AT THE BEACH, HITLER'S ART, AND A BOY NAMED PABLO

Imagine a guy at the beach: hot-pink trunks, shirtless, and with sunscreen slathered on his nose. As his kids work on building sandcastles in the sunny, 75-degree weather, he sips on an Arnold Palmer (with a little umbrella in his glass). Oh, and he's holding a Samsonite black leather briefcase.

You might think, *This guy has lost the plot.*

But haven't our smartphones become our new briefcases?

Not only do people carry their phone with them to work—they carry it *everywhere*. And if they should forget and leave it behind, it feels as though someone has yanked the pacifier from the mouth of a child.

Panic.

We are now able to carry our "briefcase" with us on vacation without it feeling as strange as it should. And we are constantly checking our emails. We wouldn't want to miss anything, would we?

In former times, nobody opened their letters before they crawled out of bed. Now many of us roll over and check our email first thing. Imagine how silly it would look to be snuggling under a blanket of open mail and a heap of letters every morning.

No wonder we don't sleep very well these days.

The internet is delivering mail to you 24/7. And if you give in to the temptation to keep checking your inbox, it messes with your circadian rhythm. Biologically, you operate in cycles. When you first wake up your body is firing cortisol, which gradually tapers off as the day goes on. Cortisol is like adrenaline, equipping you with the energy you need to go about your day. Then, later in the evening, as the sun goes down, your body—ideally—starts releasing melatonin, anticipating the end of the day when you will drift into a deep sleep.

At least that is how it is supposed to work.

When you check your emails at midnight, it throws your body into a confused tailspin as your inner clock whirls out of control. Then you don't sleep as well, and you approach the next day without the kind of rest you need for physical and emotional well-being.

We do our best work in the morning because our brain's prefrontal cortex (the part of the brain responsible for creative thinking) is most active immediately upon waking. But our obsession with emails and social media throws everything off kilter.

((((( )))))

Okay, so the smartphone isn't like the villain in a B-movie—simply evil and out to do us harm. But if we become addicted to it, it tends to have the effect of a drug. Our phone becomes a huge distraction that will keep us from focusing on the task before us or accomplishing our best work.

Doing your best work can be a real deterrent to depression. Doing something you love and are passionate about will do wonders for your frame of mind. So, don't let your technology distract you from what's important to you.

Distraction is the problem of our age.

((((( )))))

I believe that the forces of darkness work hard to get us distracted from our calling and our craft. They'll use any means necessary. Sometimes it's easier to start World War II than to keep focused on our craft. Hitler originally set out to be an artist. He took his inheritance and moved to Vienna to live and study, applying to the prestigious Academy of Fine Arts and later the School of Architecture. He wasn't good enough to be accepted. Ever seen any of his paintings? Neither have I! He gave up on art and started a war.

Contrast that with Pablo Picasso. He was such a prodigy, so skilled beyond his age, that he was making oil paintings by age 9. By age 16 he had a skill like the great Raphael, and he knew it. He drew fast. Later in life someone timed him and found he could draw a dove in 16 seconds. That 16 seconds had 6 decades of work behind it.

If you want to be on the right side of history, don't let anything distract you from your calling.

((((( )))))

Donald Miller once wrote on his blog: "No culture in history has been more distracted. If you are wondering why there are no more C.S. Lewis' in the world, no more stories as good as Tolkien's, no more cathedrals as great as the gothic's, no music as moving as Pachelbel's, it may be because the writers of these books, the tellers of these stories, the architects of these buildings and the composers of these symphonies are sitting on their couches watching television. I wonder what's on tonight."

I can't put it any better than that. Besides, I need to check Twitter.

THERE'S MUSIC
IN THE CLOUDS AND A
BONFIRE IN THE SKY

Do you know anyone who doesn't like music?

I mean, think about it. I've never met anyone who doesn't like any kind of music. Some people might dislike rap or pop or Indian sitars or country or bluegrass. Some people don't care for Coldplay or John Mayer or DMB or whatever. But no one hates music on principle.

There's a neurological reason for this. One of the things that makes music appealing is that it has a foundation built upon repetition of some kind of beat. Our prefrontal cortex enjoys anticipating the rhythm of a beat. We know what is coming next and we groove to it. We dance, move our bodies, clap, and tap our toes in time. We are moving in time with the music and celebrating our successful prediction of the next downbeat. Our brains like to make predictions and be right!

Which is why we love music.

Now, think about this: Jesus was born surrounded by music.

In ancient Israel, when a baby boy was born, the local musicians would gather near the house where the birth was to take place. They would tune up their instruments, and when the actual birth was announced, they would break into music and song.

But because Jesus was born in a stable in Bethlehem, far away from his parents' hometown, there was no group of earthly musicians waiting to strike up the band. Even though it was customary for a ditty to be played, Mary and Joseph were strangers in the area where the birth took place. So, when the earthly musicians were not on hand to celebrate, the heavenly choir of angels sang in their stead. As the Bible pictures it, there was a rip-roaring concert right there in the night sky over the fields of Bethlehem. In ancient times, when a king's son was born, a bonfire was lit on earth. When Jesus was born, a bonfire was in the sky—glory shone round the angels because He was the Son of the King of Heaven. Hey, every concert needs a light show.

Gloria!

And when Jesus was nearing the time of His crucifixion, He gathered His disciples to partake of the Lord's Supper. When they were done, the Gospels tell us, they all sang a hymn together (Matthew 26:30; Mark 14:26).

The book of Job tells us that the angels sang when God created the world (Job 38:4-7), and they sang when the world was repaired (Luke 2:13-14). And J.R.R. Tolkien imagined that Middle Earth was sung into existence by the angelic hosts.

One of my favorite verses of Scripture is Zephaniah 3:17, which says that God rejoices and sings over you and me. In the Hebrew language, the picture here is of a spinning top. Think about that. God *dances* and sings when He thinks about you and me! Such a profound and beautiful picture.

(((( ))))

Your vibe may be pop. It may be jazz. It's been said that pop artists play three chords for a thousand people…and that jazz musicians play a thousand chords for three people.

And then there is music that defies any category, like that of the Grateful Dead. As its former lead singer once said, "Don't just be the best at what you do; be the only one who does what you do." Good motto.

((((( )))))

My point is that we were made for music. In the beginning was the sound. Our souls are still reverberating from the first black hole explosion.

So, let whatever kind of music is your jam lift your heart and lift your spirit.

Add your own voice to the cosmic orchestra.

((((( )))))

Paul says that we are a *poiema* (the Greek word for poem) that reflects God's image; masterpieces which reflect Him (Ephesians 2:10). Which means we are all artists at heart. It's our calling to steward the song that is inside us. The world needs the gift you have to give. The cosmic orchestra just won't sound quite right if your contribution isn't in the mix.

So, whether you are on stage, living the dream in the bright lights, teaching chemistry to eleven-year-olds, strategizing policy in the White House, or maybe perfecting that swirl of cream as a barista, do it all for the glory of God. The word "glory" in the original languages of the Bible literally means "weight" or "excellence." If you perform any task with excellence, God will put all His weight behind you. For

God is glorified when we lift our own song and join in the celebration of creation.

((((( )))))

According to string theory, the universe is made up of elements more complicated than a point particle. Its elements are built on strings. This is how they can come into existence out of nowhere. Picture it this way: If you sing a perfect *d* note, the *d* string on the cello across the room will vibrate in answer to your voice. So too the vibrating strings of other dimensions pop particles into existence just as the cello strings bring notes into the air. What does all this mean?

The universe is built on music. Just as a pulsar tends to hum a steady e-flat note, and the angels are singing at creation, so too the vibrating strings of the cosmos are, in effect, a song.

((((( )))))

Nothing brings more glory to God than when you just *send it* and blow everyone away with your talents.

So, give it all you've got. The world needs your contribution. Go be the rock star you were always meant to be.

Don't die with your song still inside you.

DON'T DRINK THE BOOS

Failure is okay.

Babe Ruth was one of the most prolific home run hitters in the history of baseball. On his way to breaking records, he also struck out 1,330 times. He didn't let failure stop him from being the Great Bambino and the Sultan of Swat. The naysayers couldn't deter him from swinging for the fences every time he stepped up to the plate. Ruth once quipped, "The loudest boos come from the cheapest seats." His all-in approach that accepted the likelihood of occasional failure was what made him one of baseball's legends.

If you are going to fail, fail spectacularly. Fail greatly. Fail with a smile on your face. Fail in the process of putting forth your best effort. If you are going to fail, fail forward. The hero is never the cold and timid soul who plays it safe, but the one who risks everything and isn't afraid of a few failures on his résumé. You can't know victory if you've never actually tried. You can't know victory if you've never known defeat.

Beyond this present failure may well be your greatest moment of achievement.

(((( ))))

By the way, how many statues have you seen that are erected to honor the critics and naysayers?

((((( )))))

In *Optimisfits*, I refer to some examples from Mel Robbins's *The 5 Second Rule*:

> Do you know the game Angry Birds? Rovio, the brand that created the game launched fifty-one unsuccessful games before they developed Angry Birds. How about the Avengers star Mark Ruffalo? Do you know how many auditions he did before he landed his first role? Almost 600! Even Babe Ruth struck out 1,330 times. My favorite vacuum cleaner is Dyson…James Dyson created 5,127 prototypes. What? And this last one will blow your mind. Picasso created nearly 100 masterpieces in his lifetime. But what most people don't know is that he created a total of more than 50,000 works of art. 50,000. That's two pieces of art a day.[1]

So, when you hear your critics scoffing about your strikeouts and your failures, don't drink the boos.

Remember, they are sitting up in the stands, but you are on the field!

THE INITIAL
SINGULARITY

God is not at war with science. He invented it.

A lot of people seem to think that the more science progresses, the less it needs God to explain the mysteries around us. My friend, the truth is just the opposite.

Here's an example. We know that the universe is expanding. How? Because we can document that the galaxies are all moving away from each other…and they are picking up speed in the process. We know this because researchers have used radio telescopes to record the phenomenon of the red shift, which is like figuring out how fast an ambulance is moving away from you by listening to the fading wail of its siren. Only in this case, we are dealing with light waves rather than sound waves. If you use mathematical formulas to run this backwards, like you'd rewind a film, you'll find that eventually everything converges at a single point, which the scientists call the "initial singularity." This singularity, they propose, was an extremely condensed state of matter, one where everything in the entire universe would fit into a space smaller than a sugar cube.

In a great burst of light and power, every galaxy, star, planet, human being, and quark had its beginning. Some have called this "the big bang." Before that moment when it all came into being, our laws of gravity, electromagnetism, and the weak and strong nuclear forces were just one unified force field. Time probably didn't exist in the initial singularity. The clock wasn't ticking…and it wasn't not ticking. But all the potential for everything was right there in our figurative sugar cube.

And then, to quote the book of Genesis, "God said…"

Scientists pretty much agree that whatever caused this cosmic explosion of existence is infinite and unnamable. But we know better. We know that Mystery as the Great Prime Mover, the Creator, God.

((((( )))))

Then along came Einstein, who showed that everything we call "solid" in our existence is actually made up of primal nuclear elements whirling around each other in mostly empty space. What little mass there is only has existence because some particles interact with an *invisible* and *universal* field called the "Higgs Field." The reason you and I are physical beings is because most of our body's particles create a quantum drag against the Higgs field that makes them slow down from light speed and gain mass in the process. Wild, huh?

Cosmology depicts a force that created us and then transformed itself into a system of forces and energy that sustain the universe. And there is God at the center of it all, the Creator and Sustainer of everything that exists.

If that isn't God, then I'll eat my hand. Or a sugar cube.

FORGET THE MUD

One thing I have learned from the crazy pace I keep in my life these days is how much I need rest. It's kind of hard for me to shut down and shut off. But if I don't do that from time to time, I will pay the price. If, like me, you don't want to rust out or burn out, you must take some time to *receive* if you are going to have the resources to *give*.

Unless you get recharged from time to time, your battery just gets more and more depleted. Pretty soon you are empty.

Sometimes you must stand still to see the salvation of the Lord.

A lot of people end up depressed because they run out of juice and can no longer function emotionally. They need some rest so that they can start paying attention to the things that really matter in their life. There's a good reason why God made the need for rest (the Sabbath) one of the Ten Commandments.

Jesus embodied the Sabbath. Did you know that according to Jewish law you not only weren't supposed to work on the Sabbath, but you couldn't even do something as simple as making clay? Making clay was considered work, which was forbidden on the Sabbath day. In Egypt, the Israelites made clay for Pharaoh's pyramids, enjoying no Sabbath, slaving away for four centuries. So, Jesus really stirred things up when He healed the man born blind on the Sabbath by spitting on some dirt and making clay and then applying it to the man's eyes. This was one way Jesus showed Himself to be the Lord of the Sabbath. Think about it. For 400 years the children of Israel had been slaves in Egypt, and they had no day of rest from laboring for the Egyptians. In a sense, Jesus made clay so that the Israelites didn't have to. They could enter their rest and enjoy their Sabbath.

Jesus showed His people that when we work, God rests. But when we rest, God works.

It's only when we stop and stand still that we can see God at work. Remember the story about Moses and the burning bush? The rabbis tell us that the bush didn't suddenly start burning when Moses stumbled upon it. No, it had been burning the whole time. Moses was simply moving slowly enough and paying enough attention that he *noticed* it. He didn't have his head down, looking at his phone every six minutes like most of us do. He was awake and aware.

Sometimes I have my shoulders hunched and my head down, and I miss the miracles burning on the side of the road and the moments of magic occurring all around me. My eyes are too glued to my screen and my hand is stuck on the proverbial plow.

If you will unplug and get the rest you need, a burning bush might just appear to remind you that freedom has come, that your bondage is over, and that God has prepared a promised land for you.

((((( )))))

The Jews tell an ancient legend about two men walking through the Red Sea during the exodus. They started complaining about the mud between their toes while the glassy watery walls of their liberation rose up around them.

We need to forget the mud and meditate on the miracles.

((((( )))))

I find comfort from the life of a great preacher, Charles Spurgeon. He suffered from depression in his heart and gout in his feet, but neither thing stopped him from serving God. He had a megachurch in London before anyone ever thought to call it that. He was famed for his sermons, which were often made into bestselling books.

Once, he was up late at night trying to finish one of these masterful sermons but couldn't quite seem to nail it. His wife suggested that he go to bed and get some sleep, and then wake early the next morning so he could finish it. He shuffled off to bed and soon fell asleep. But as he slept, he began preaching in his sleep—the very sermon he had been struggling with. His wife grabbed a pad of paper and began to take notes.

In the morning, she showed them to him. "Why, that's exactly what I wanted to say!" he exclaimed.

No wonder they called him the "prince of preachers." He could preach even in his sleep!

Literally.

One of my favorite things he ever wrote was this: "If you were to take out of the Scriptures all the stories that have to do with poor, afflicted men and women, what a very small book the Bible would become, especially if together with the stories you removed all the psalms of the sorrowful, all the promises for the distressed, and all the passages which belong to the children of grief."[1]

Maybe if you'll find the time for a little rest, you'll find that God will supply exactly what you need for right now.

Noticed any burning bushes lately?

SURFING THE WONDERS

A story has been told of Napoleon Bonaparte and his entourage sailing along the Mediterranean Sea. The topic of conversation for his crew was whether God existed. Most of the people in the ship, influenced by the current Enlightenment-thought of their day, were adamant in their assertion that God did not exist, and that belief in Him was just an emotional crutch for the ignorant masses. Napoleon was silent as he listened to their arguments, until he finally interrupted the flow of their disputations. He simply lifted his hand toward the sky, followed by a sweeping gesture across the landscape of sea and sky.

"Gentlemen," Napoleon asked, "who made all of this?"

I believe, along with that famous Frenchman, that it takes more faith to be an atheist than it does to believe in a Creator, whose Divine intelligence can be seen at work in the world He created.

((((( ))))))

My favorite painting is Vincent van Gogh's *The Starry Night*. Its magnificence cannot be argued, with its ingenious use of breathtaking color and swirling brushstrokes. Now, what do I see when my eyes travel across the across the canvas? Is it just a byproduct of a fortuitous accident of oil paint? Or, is it the result of the wild creativity of van Gogh? Does not every brushstroke speak of his intelligence and inner life?

Similarly, does not the whole created universe also reveal the hand of an imaginatively powerful and wildly creative Creator?

One cannot long remain jaded when one wanders among the wonders of the world around us.

There are koalas munching on eucalyptus leaves, foxes sneaking about ever so slyly, and sloths doing whatever it is that sloths do.

In *What We Talk About When We Talk About God*, Rob Bell shares this:

> Earth weighs about six billion trillion tons, is moving around the sun at roughly sixty-six thousand miles an hour, and is doing this while rotating at the equator at a little over a thousand miles an hour. So when you feel like your head is spinning, it is. Paris is, after all, going six hundred miles an hour.
>
> Earth's surface is made up of about ten big plates and twenty smaller ones that never stop slipping and sliding, like Greenland, which moves half an inch a year. The general estimate is that this current configuration of continents that we know to be Africa, Asia, Europe, etc. has been like this about a tenth of 1 percent of history. The world, as we know it, is a relatively new arrangement.
>
> Every day there are on average two earthquakes somewhere in the world that measure 2 or greater on the Richter scale, every second about one hundred lightning bolts hit the ground, and every nineteen seconds someone sitting in a restaurant hears Lionel Richie's song "Dancing on the Ceiling" one. more. time.[1]

How does all that strike you? Doesn't it activate a sense of wonder and enchantment which awakens the soul to sing?

Don't be overwhelmed by the massiveness of the earth. Be encouraged by its magic.

It's all a tapestry. You miss the beauty if you stare too closely at each thread. Instead, step back and let yourself be overcome with awe.

Just go with it. Surf the wonders.

(((( ))))

G.K. Chesterton said it so well: "Poets do not go mad; but chess-players do. Mathematicians go mad, and cashiers; but creative artists very seldom…Poetry is sane because it floats easily in an infinite sea; reason seeks to cross the infinite sea, and so make it finite. The result is mental exhaustion…To accept everything is an exercise, to understand everything a strain…The poet asks to get his head into the heavens. It is the logician who seeks to get the heavens into his head. And it is his head that splits."[2]

My hat goes off to the mathematician who tries to bridge the infinite… but I think it rather more pleasant to be the poet who simply swims in it.

((((( )))))

There are approximately 5,000 stars visible to the naked eye and more than a septillion that we cannot see. As well as 170 billion in our galaxy.[3] Amazing. Isaiah tells us that God calls out the stars by name (Isaiah 40:26). Epsilon, Antares, and G2 Dwarf. But even more amazing is that the same God whom the Bible says counts the stars (Psalm 147:4 NASB) also counts the hairs of my head (Matthew 10:30). And that the Good Shepherd also calls His sheep by name (John 10:3). In the Old Testament, the sheep had to die for the sins of the shepherd, and in the New Testament, the Good Shepherd dies for the sins of the sheep.

How do we miss all this mystery? Why are so few of us truly ablaze with the wonder of Ultimate Reality and the Thing behind the things?

How many miracles do we miss because we have our heads down, our eyes glued to a screen as we compare our lives with one another on Instagram?

((((( )))))

Real beauty is not found in flash-in-the pan Instagram stars, but in the stars sparkling in the heavens above. Our greatest riches are not in diamonds but in the gems glistening on the sea during a fiery-orange sunset. We live in a bounteous universe of supernovas and a giant swirl of stars and penguins. So, God wants to remove our jaded, cynical, postmodern lenses on the world and replace them with the wonder of living with Him in this magical universe He created.

This world is more like Narnia than a mathematical equation. When we regain this perspective, we can more easily pass through the wardrobe.

If the wonder inside you has diminished from when you were a child, and you've settled for a life spent searching for significance on social media, then I have news for you.

God wants to transform your hollow hopes into real ones.

((((( )))))

In Ephesians 3:8, Paul writes of "the unsearchable riches of Christ" (KJV). My favorite exposition of this phrase comes from a nineteenth-century pastor of the London Metropolitan Church named Charles Spurgeon.

Here is a chap who could wax lyrical. So much that you may need to read this paragraph a couple of times to suck all the marrow from it. But the payoff is grand.

My Master has riches beyond the count of arithmetic, the measurement of reason, the dream of imagination, or the eloquence of words. They are *unsearchable*! You may look, and study, and weigh, but Jesus is a greater Saviour than you think Him to be when your thoughts are at the greatest. My Lord is more ready to pardon than you to sin, more able to forgive than you to transgress. My Master is more willing to supply your wants than you are to confess them. Never tolerate low thoughts of my Lord Jesus. When you put the crown on His head, you will only crown Him with silver when He deserves gold. *My Master has riches of happiness to bestow upon you now.* He can make you to lie down in green pastures, and lead you beside still waters. There is no music like the music of His pipe, when He is the Shepherd and you are the sheep, and you lie down at His feet. There is no love like His, neither earth nor heaven can match it. To know Christ and to be found in Him—oh! this is life, this is joy, this is marrow and fatness, wine on the lees well refined. My Master does not treat His servants churlishly; He gives to them as a king giveth to a king; He gives them two heavens—a heaven below in serving Him here, and a heaven above in delighting in Him forever. *His unsearchable riches will be best known in eternity.* He will give you on the way to heaven all you need; your place of defence shall be the munitions of rocks, your bread shall be given you, and your waters shall be sure; but it is there, THERE, where you shall hear the song of them that triumph, the shout of them that feast, and shall have a face-to-face view of the glorious and beloved One. The unsearchable riches of Christ! This is the tune for the minstrels of earth, and the song for the harpers of heaven. Lord, teach us more and more of Jesus, and we will tell out the good news to others."[4]

The angels sang when God made the world, and the Muses still sing today.

He who has an ear to hear let him hear.

The way to conquer this waterlogged mote of dust is to float amongst its wonders.

OCTOPUSES
AND PIZZA SLICES

Unless you can juggle like an octopus or divide yourself up like a pizza, there's no way you can do all the multitasking our culture requires of us. While our brains can focus on 4-7 things at any given moment, none of us can keep up with the seemingly endless tasks on our to-do list.

One of the common causes of depression and discouragement is the feeling of being overwhelmed—as though too many things are going on in our lives. We might feel we are barely keeping all the balls in the air when suddenly we find ourselves having to juggle six more.

There is too much to be done. Too many tasks, too many future projects, and way too many commitments. The stress multiplies, and we feel that we have so much to do that we can't do anything!

Here is some good news. God has a better way. The Bible propagates a "one thing" mentality.

"ONE THING I ask from the LORD" said David, "…that I may dwell in the house of the Lord all the days of my life" (Psalm 27:4).

"ONE THING is needful," Jesus said to the overtaxed Martha. "And

Mary hath chosen that good part" (Luke 10:42 kjv). For while Martha fussed about what needed to be done to make everything perfect for her guest, Mary simply plopped down at His feet, hanging on to every word of wisdom He offered. She wasn't going to miss a moment.

Jesus told the rich young ruler: "ONE THING you lack. Go, sell everything you have and give to the poor, and you will have treasure in heaven" (Mark 10:21).

"ONE THING I do," wrote Paul, "forgetting what is behind and straining toward what is ahead, I press on toward the goal to win the prize for which God has called me" (Philippians 3:13-14).

The Bible is all about the ONE THING.

One of the ways you can defeat stress and anxiety and depression in your life is to embrace this ONE THING mentality.

Make the first step. Accomplish what is in front of you. That's all you really have power over anyway. When you do that, each of the other steps to take will fall into place in their time.

This is one of the reasons why Navy SEALs are so strong. During hell week they go through 96 hours of sleep deprivation, and they put their bodies through excruciating workouts. They push themselves to the limit. There is only one way for them to get through this ordeal: They teach themselves to focus on one task at a time. If, while they do moving push-ups, they worry about how they will have to lift giant logs next, they will collapse under the pressure. But the SEALs who graduate successfully are the ones who discipline their minds to focus upon the *present* task, and that is the key to getting through all their otherwise overwhelming trials.

You can become an effective soldier of the Lord by becoming like the SEALs. Focus on the ONE THING that God puts in front of you. Develop a minimalist mind—ONE THING at a time. It'll help you cope with the burdens that others place on you and that you place on yourself.

Remember what Jesus said: "My yoke is easy, and my burden is light" (Matthew 11:30). He doesn't call you to stress out about the million things you have to do. God has called you to a ONE THING mentality. When this becomes your focus, you'll be like Paul and David and Jesus, and you'll accomplish more than you ever dreamed—and you'll do it more peacefully than you ever imagined.

That is the ONE THING you should never forget!

THE TWO MOST
IMPORTANT QUESTIONS

It was a dark and stormy night.

Hey, I've always wanted to start a chapter that way.

So, now that I have your attention, let me tell you the story of Akiva, who was heading home from a long journey on such a night about two thousand years ago. Akiva was widely esteemed as the wisest man of his time. People would come from near and far to hear him speak and dispense his wisdom.

On this particular night, the fog had become so thick that he couldn't see very well as he made his way down the dark road. In the swampy gloom he missed the turn to his village, and instead of heading right, he turned left. This took him to the gates of a huge Roman military outpost, where he made himself known.

A voice rang out from the top of the wall of the garrison: "Who are you and what are you doing here?"

"Excuse me?" said Akiva.

"Who are you and what are you doing here?" came the voice again.

Akiva paused for a moment and then said, "How much are they pay-ing you?"

"What?" asked the guard.

Akiva repeated the question.

The guard answered, "Twenty denarii a week."

"Well," said Akiva, "I'll pay you twice as much to come to my house each morning and ask me those two questions."

((((( )))))

Those are the two questions you should ask yourself every morning.

"Who am I?"

"What am I doing here?"

((((( )))))

This is how I would answer them:

"I am a child of God."

"I'm here to give hope to the world."

This is my passion and the thing that drives me to do everything I do.

How about you?

WHEN HOLIDAYS
ARE HARD

Thanksgiving and Christmas can be two of the hardest seasons to be happy and grateful. For some, they are a depression magnet. One survey showed that 38 percent of people report having more stress during the holidays.[1] Being around families and loved ones who are excited to gather together can exacerbate your feeling of being alone in your pain. Many of us can feel like an outsider during these family celebrations.

When you start to feel this way, remember that Jesus Himself was an outsider. Hey, He wasn't even invited to His own birthday party. When He was born, there was no room for Him in the inn. Early church fathers and historians, like Ephiphanius and Origen, all believed He was born in a cave and then laid in a feeding trough. Not a prestigious beginning. He didn't get the typical welcome from local musicians, which was supposed to be the case when a baby boy was born. There was no one there to strike up the band. The only music was the lowing of the cattle and the whinny of the donkey.

But as we discussed, where the musicians failed, the heavenly angels burst forth in their stead. They gave a concert that would put Coldplay to shame! They sang "Glory to God in the highest!" Think about it. Can you imagine the angels popping up like stars in the heavenly realms? (These angels were maybe the first pop stars?)

And remember who the recipients of this gala musical extravaganza were. It wasn't held in the local amphitheater or broadcast live for the masses. It wasn't an exclusive ticket for the upper classes. It was for a bunch of shepherds. In those times shepherds were looked down upon. They were the outcasts of society. Sometimes literally so. If you broke the rules or didn't fit in, sometimes they would send you out to tend the goats and the lambs. Because living among the animals left you with a particularly unpleasant scent, there was no hiding your lowly place in the social pecking order. It was for just this crowd of misfits that the angels sang of the good news of Jesus's birth.

(((( ))))

So, isn't it interesting that Jesus used a shepherd as a symbol and word picture for God's care for us, just as David did in the twenty-third psalm? Jesus referred to Himself as "the Good Shepherd" (John 10:14), and it became one of the most familiar representations of Christ in the art of the early church. He watches over us like that shepherd who carries the lamb upon his shoulders—safe, secure, and protected.

But people didn't think too highly of shepherds in ancient Israel. They were always under suspicion of being crooks and thieves, so their testimony was considered worthless in court. And working all day with sheep left you with the recognizable odor of your flock. Whenever they came to town, their smell would precede them. It was better for knowing they were coming than having a bell around their necks!

Some scholars have proposed that the shepherds who came to visit the newborn king were those responsible for taking care of the flocks owned by the temple. These were lambs destined to be sacrificed for sin. So, the shepherds who watched over the sacrificial lambs followed the angels to see the Lamb of God.

He sacrificed His temple (His body) to make us temples for the Holy

Spirit, places where God can dwell. This indwelling is the whole point. Not the kind of religion that Christian Smith calls "moralistic therapeutic deism," which is essentially the idea that religion consists of living a good life, finding your personal happiness, and giving a nod toward a God who isn't really involved in human lives.[2] This kind of belief in a distant and legalistic God makes the holidays not only meaningless but also sad.

((((( )))))

So, when you feel like you aren't fitting in, remember that the Good Shepherd was an outcast too.

There might not be any room at the inn, but in His Father's house are many rooms (John 14:2).

((((( )))))

Rejoice even in the midst of your rejection, for you are a lamb in the loving care of the Good Shepherd.

When you are left out, consider it an opportunity to stand out.

The boy who was not invited to His own birthday party wants to give you a second birth.

WELCOME TO HOGWARTS, YOU MUGGLES

When I look at the world around me, I'm always filled with wonder.

I can understand clearly what David was thinking when he wrote psalms that praise God for the beauty and order and mystery of the world around us. I have felt that too. And the closer you get to the stars, the more mysterious it all becomes.

Think about the universe and how magical it really is. Let's take a brief journey to recount its surprises.

In the middle of our own galaxy, the Milky Way, is a supermassive black hole that's four million times greater than the mass of our sun.[1] And our sun, parenthetically, is so large that you could fit 1.3 million Earths into it if you ever took a notion to do such a thing.[2] This black hole's gravity is so strong that it not only hurls stars into mind-bogglingly swift orbits but also warps time itself. According to the theory of relativity (which our iPhones actually depend upon for the determination of our GPS positions), if you had a son and left him on Earth while you went to live near a black hole by yourself for a time (though I'm not sure if there are any Realtors who could get you financing for that new home there), when you returned to Earth your kid would actually be older than you are. Yup. Welcome to Hogwarts, you muggles!

Or consider this: There is a volcano on Mars. It is so tall that it dwarfs Mt. Everest in height. No big deal, right? In fact, our own moon shows evidence of once having volcanic activity as well. There goes the neighborhood.

There is a supermassive black hole called Sagittarius A. Its gravity well is so strong that it hurls a nearby star (S2) into a mind-bogglingly swift orbit (2% light speed), and it actually warps space-time.

Jupiter has a whole bunch of moons. Those close to the planet are in a constant state of flux and are oblong, being slowly torn apart by the gravity of this massive sphere.[3] Jupiter itself is what they call a gas giant, meaning that it's made up of the same stuff as our sun. It's so big that if you increased its mass by 80 times, it would turn into a star. The giant red spot on Jupiter is actually an anticyclone that's been swirling for at least 350 years.[4] Wild!

What about shooting stars, like those you might sometimes see streaking across the night sky? We'd assume from the way they light things up that they are very large, but the truth is that some of them are actually the size of a grain of sand. The comet that burns up as it enters our atmosphere might just be small enough that it would fit in the palm of your hand.[5]

(((( ))))

Thinking about space baptizes my imagination!

(((( ))))

To keep depression at bay, we need to have our eyes reopened to wonder.

We must leave some room for the miraculous in our lives, some room for adventure, some room for a little magic and mystery.

Science is great. I love science. But sometimes science goes wrong when it tries to explain away all the wonder and enchantment of life. That isn't science; it's scientism, the belief that everything can be explained through a mathematical equation or an experiment. Pretty quickly these explanations turn into a process of *explaining away*.

Some would have us believe that everything is predetermined by our biology. That we are the puppets of the ongoing evolution of the cosmos. That we know full well what kind of tricks the universe might be playing on us when our back is turned.

I refuse to accept such a hopeless way of seeing things.

We need the magic and the miracles.

More than that, we need the Miracle Worker.

((((( )))))

Are you suffering from a little seasonal affective disorder due to the gloomy weather here on Earth? Wish you could soar to the stars for a little relief? Well, be careful what you wish for, because it rains on other planets in our solar system. "Rain on Venus is made of sulfuric acid, and due to the intense heat it evaporates before it even reaches the surface."[6] So maybe you won't need an umbrella after all.

In *What We Talk About When We Talk About God*, Rob Bell says,

> The edge of the universe is roughly ninety billion trillion miles away (*roughly* being the word you use when your estimate could be off by A MILLION MILES), the visible universe is a million million million million miles across, and all of the galaxies in the

universe are moving away from all of the other galaxies in the universe at the same time…The solar system that we live in, which fills less than a trillionth of available space, is moving at 558 thousand miles per hour. It's part of the Milky Way galaxy, and it takes our solar system between 200 and 250 million years to orbit the Milky Way galaxy *once*.[7]

If you are seriously pondering a relocation to find better weather, I suggest you don't leave Earth for too long. An astronaut's time in space has to be limited because of the effect it has on our bodies. Spend too much time out in the cosmos, and your risk of cancer tends to skyrocket (pun intended) due to genetic damage from cosmic rays.

The sun is out there spewing dangerous radiation, but thankfully our planet's atmosphere blocks it out. God has made a good provision there.

Yes, it's a wacky, wild, weird, and wonderful universe that came from the hand of God. Hey, this place is as magical as Hogwarts or Narnia!

PROMISES, PROMISES

Here is one of the best weapons against depression you are ever going to find...

Next to every one of God's promises, just write the word "mine."

The Bible isn't a rule book; it's a hope book. It's chock-full of promises you need to hear and believe.

Here are just a few:

- You are hard-pressed on every side, but not crushed (2 Corinthians 4:8).

- He gives you beauty for ashes (Isaiah 61:3).

- The Lord your God is a sun and a shield, and He will withhold no good thing from those who love Him (Psalm 84:11).

- If you sow in tears, you will reap in joy (Psalm 126:5).

- If you pass through the fire, you will not be burned (Isaiah 43:2).

- Return to your fortress, you prisoners of hope; even now

I announce that I will restore twice as much to you (Zechariah 9:12).

- Delight yourself in the Lord, and He will give you the desires of your heart (Psalm 37:4).

- Joy comes with the morning (Psalm 30:5).

These are some of the more than 3,500 promises in the Bible. Go get out the Good Book and start finding more of them. Fear is faith in the devil's promises, but hope looks beyond the immediate evidence of our problems to the fulfillment of God's promises.

One of the chief things that helped me through depression was clinging to the promises of God. He's made a lot of promises you can hold on to…as you hold on to Him.

POMEGRANATES, TASSELS, AND HEALING WINGS

It's difficult for modern Americans to grasp what Paul and theologians are really talking about when they use the word "grace."

Our republic is a capitalist society predicated upon lobbying and campaigning, success through competition, and climbing the corporate ladder through hard work. It's a version of Darwin's survival of the fittest, where everyone is scrambling after the consumer's money. Our work ethic emphasizes that we all must earn our keep and not be a drag on the economic system. A great myth is that men and women are able, through much hard work, to pull themselves up by their own bootstraps. (Parenthetical thought: If your boots happen to have bootstraps, have you ever actually tried to pull yourself up by grabbing hold of them? I don't believe it can actually be done. So much for this myth of self-reliance...) The whole system is based upon reaching the top by elevating ourselves over our competition through working harder than the next guy.

So we push and strive and advertise to get ahead. We adapt and overcome. We burn the candle at both ends. Add all this together, and you have the recipe for success.

But, the Kingdom of God isn't a free enterprise system.

In fact, the *less* you work to achieve God's grace, the better things will go.

In America, you have to want it, work for it, and deserve it. Grace runs counter to the American capitalist system, which is why grace is hard for us to really comprehend.

God's love cannot be earned or finagled or bought. It's free. No strings attached.

Receiving God's love is like sleeping or being sincere; when it comes to grace, the less you *try*, the better it works.

Which is really good news.

(((( )))))

Don't get me wrong. I'm a big advocate for working hard. That's one of the things that helped me climb out of my depression. Before original sin was original blessing. God called work "good." Working isn't the result of the fall. Adam was called to be a gardener long before the events with the "apple." Work is holy. Like our first father, we are all created to value hard work. It's good for you. And it helps you achieve your dreams. Remember what I said earlier about the 10,000-hour rule? Generally, I hate rules, but this one has freed me to pursue a purpose in my life. You can look at successful people and usually find they are successful because they put in the time and effort to get good at their calling in life.

So, yes. If you want to make an impact, don't be afraid to work it as hard as you can.

But...

(((( )))))

What is true for dreams isn't true for God's love.

It's so easy to get the two mixed up.

To gain God's favor you have to...do nothing. Just reach out and accept it.

It requires zero work.

Of course, that doesn't sit very well with us. After all, isn't religion all about trying to please God by being a good person and doing good things? And isn't the idea of needing a free handout or free lunch a sign of weakness and dependency? Grace can't possibly be that easy, can it? We have to do our part, right?

Wrong. Working for grace is counterproductive. When you work, God rests; when you rest, God works. He'll let you spin your spiritual wheels if you really want to, but He'd rather take care of you through His grace.

The theme of the book of Hebrews is this: Labor to enter in to rest. We are to work on learning how to rest.

When Jesus breathed out His last words from the cross, they were: "It is finished!" (John 19:30 NASB). The work of love had been accomplished.

Paul uses the first half of the book of Ephesians to remind people of who they are—no commands attached. Then he spends the second half of the book telling people what life looks like when we believe the truths of the first half. *Activity flows from identity*, not the other way around. He even warns them not to try to finish in their own strength and effort what was begun by grace. The whole process is grace; it's a gift. Many people think we are justified by grace and sanctified by works. In my humble and correct opinion, and I say this with all due disrespect—that is wrong!

On the next page you'll find some solid theology.

- We are justified by grace.

- We are sanctified by grace.

- We are glorified by grace.

Yes, it's all grace. Not, we do a part and He does a part. He is doing it all.

((((( )))))

Frankly, you *deserve* grace. I know some of you are thinking, *Wait, he just went over the edge.* But you do. The fact that He made you means He should take care of you. I don't like those worship songs that say things like "I don't deserve Your love." That's like a baby saying to its mother, "I don't deserve your milk." We don't have to earn God's love. We are His creation. We are part of His family. The issue is not *worth*, but *birth*.

We need to stop thinking in terms of "earning" or "deserving" altogether. God's love is our right as His children. He created us, and it's His job to care for us. Which He does. That is the bottom line.

So, if God's love is yours because you are His kid, then you need to stop thinking that you need to do more to earn that affection. The whole plan of salvation isn't about a heavenly courtroom where a legal transaction took place, but about taking off your shoes because you are in the living room of the Most High—which is holy ground.

When Paul wrote that "godliness with contentment is great gain" (1 Timothy 6:6), the word picture he is using in the Greek language is that of a child resting peacefully in the arms of a father. We are not meant to be on the receiving end of the whipcrack of the law, which acts like a slave master driving us to a confrontation with a judge. We can rest contentedly in the arms of Abba.

((((( )))))

In Exodus 28:33-34, the law of Moses decreed that a priest was to decorate the hem of his garments with the image of pomegranates. Here's an interesting fact: The law of Moses contains 613 precepts, which is how many seeds there are in the average pomegranate. What a perfect metaphor for walking in the way of the law. That was the duty of the priest, who was the intermediary between God and the people. The word for "priest" in Latin is *pontifex*, which means "bridge builder." The priest spoke to God for the people, and he spoke to the people for God. He built the bridge.

Hebrews tells us that Jesus is our Great High Priest (Hebrews 4:14).

Both Mark and Luke tell the story of a woman who had been hemorrhaging for 12 years (Mark 5:25-34; Luke 8:43-48). This made her ceremonially unclean, so when she reached out to touch the hem of Jesus's garment, she was breaking the law. Did Jesus care that she was breaking the rules? No, He was all about love. He healed her instantaneously.

The book of Malachi says that the "Sun of righteousness [will] arise with healing in his wings" (Malachi 4:2 KJV). In the original language, the word "wings" could be translated "the hem of his garment." Sure enough, this story of healing shows the wings of Jesus's garment, the hem, pouring forth healing to the sick woman.

In addition, Numbers 15:37-41 decrees that all devout Jews were to wear robes with fringes ending in four tassels with a blue cord going through them. They were to remind a Jew every time he dressed that he was committed to keeping God's law. So, when the woman broke the law to touch the hem of Jesus's garment (which symbolized healing and the law), His healing effectively brought an end to the law (Romans 10:4).

Pomegranates, tassels, and healing wings.

Jesus didn't come to abolish the law, but to fulfill it (Matthew 5:17).

This idea of *fulfilling* rather than abolishing has some interesting background in the ancient Hebrew culture. If you butchered a text and grossly misinterpreted it, you were said to have "abolished the law." If, however, you discovered and displayed a golden nugget from the law to make a brilliant insight that correctly interpreted the Old Testament, you were said to have "fulfilled the law." This rabbinic distinction helps us understand more fully what Jesus meant. He wasn't butchering the law but explaining it, bringing forth what it really meant. He was seeking to get to the heart of the law rather than debating the letter of the law. He was bringing out the true intention of the Old Testament law.

And He "fleshed out" that law in His own person. He fulfilled it perfectly but transcended it, and ended it once and for all. *It is finished!*

He carried the 613 laws quite literally in His robe. Pomegranate vibes.

Then Paul tells us that "He who began a good work in you will carry it on to completion" (Philippians 1:6). In the Greek language that phrase—"carry it on to completion"—is *telestai*, the same word Jesus used on the cross when He shouted: "It is finished!" Just as surely as Jesus carried the cross, God will carry your purpose through to completion. He is doing the carrying, not you.

(((( ))))

Now for the rest of the story…

Eusebius, a church historian from about AD 300, tells a story about what happened later to the woman whose hemorrhaging was healed by Jesus. She was so moved by what Jesus had done for her that she, at her own cost and in her own city, erected a statue to commemorate her healing. This statue was later torn down by Julian the Apostate, a Roman emperor who wanted to bring back the pagan gods. In its place he erected a statue of himself. There is a legend that the replacement statue was then destroyed by a thunderbolt from God. How legendary is that?

The woman who was healed had good reason to celebrate, for she had to bear not only the pain of her affliction but also the ostracization that went along with it. She labored under the label "unclean," which was her designation under the Law. The Talmud gives roughly 11 cures for such a problem, one of which is carrying the ashes of an ostrich egg in a rag. The latest in medical procedures! Mark's gospel tells us that doctors had taken advantage of her; that she had spent all her money seeking a cure but had only gotten worse. (See Mark 5:26. Interestingly, when Dr. Luke wrote about the story, he omitted the phrase about getting worse. I guess he was trying to protect the integrity of his profession!)

Her faith had marginalized her as unclean. The doctors couldn't do anything to make her better. And then along came Jesus.

He ignored all the rules about not touching a person who was unclean. He healed her.

Grace reminds us that He loves us in spite of all the complexities, failures, and uncleanness in our souls.

So, rest in His love and stop trying to be the perfect Christian.

Jesus took a beating for you so you can stop beating yourself up.

A TRIBUTE TO ST. OLAF

Now, before any of you pull your copy of *Lives of the Saints* off the shelf or start a Google search, let me clarify who I am talking about when I refer to St. Olaf. He's the snowman from the movie *Frozen*.

One of the goals of my life is to become like Olaf. That little dude is more than cool—he's solid.

Olaf is friendly, outgoing, and caring. Though he's made of snow, he likes warm hugs. He has magical powers. He loves all things summer even though he's a snowman. He's a dreamer with an uncanny ability to disassemble himself at times. (That last trait, my friend, could prove useful sometimes.)

What's not to like?

Because he was built by two little girls, Olaf has never lost touch with his own childlike origins. There isn't an ounce of cynicism in his DNA.

His heart is filled with wonder, which is hardwired into his unshakable belief in love. He has some profound things to say, like "Some people are worth melting for," and "An act of love will thaw a frozen heart."

Love has a way of restoring wonder back into even the chilliest of hearts.

((((( )))))

I think kids love Jesus for some of the same reasons they love Olaf. Here was a guy who embodied love better than any snowman ever could. The grown-ups largely missed the point, and they killed Him. The kiddos never would have done that. When a bunch of these little ankle biters crowded around Him, trying to hang out with Him, the grown-ups called for a little more decorum. Jesus had a different point of view. He said, "Let the little children come to me…for the kingdom of heaven belongs to such as these" (Matthew 19:14).

Jesus also said that the only way to enter heaven was to "become like little children" (Matthew 18:3). Jesus lived this out to the full, with a toddler's zest for life. He waded out among lilies and listened to the singing of the sparrows. He saw the beauty in the world. He bathed Himself in its wonders. He didn't show much concern for respectability.

The New Testament doesn't emphasize us as grown-up men and women as much as it emphasizes that we should become children—the children of God. God is our Father, our loving Abba, our Daddy!

((((( )))))

With all the bad news floating about in the media, it's easy to become jaded and cynical and skeptical, and to squash everything childlike that resides within us.

It's time to become like Olaf.

Be a child again.

Believe in wonder. Believe in love.

My friend, don't let this world's tribulations melt your own inner Olaf.

RAM IN THE THICKET

I was recently in Europe with some of my friends, doing a shoot for my TV program. It was quite an adventure, and along the way we came up with a new phrase for the way God takes care of us.

Genesis 22 tells the story of Abraham, who, when called to sacrifice his son, is stopped at the last minute by an angel. Instead of sacrificing his firstborn, God provides an alternative—a ram in a thicket. Here God reveals Himself as "Jehovah Jireh," which means "the Lord provides." The ram symbolizes such provision. So, when there was an unexpected McDonald's (in Zurich—we were dying for some American fast food!), or when we got unexpected cell service while we were filming in the desert (the same location, by the way, where they filmed *Pirates of the Caribbean*), or when we got complimentary upgrades from our Eurail passes to a better class of service—we called such provisions a "ram in the thicket." The ram quickly became the theme of our European travels.

One night, in Zurich, we didn't have a place to stay. Like Jesus, there was no room for us at the inn. Our money was tight, and it felt as though it was 190 degrees below zero. Switzerland is known for banking, remaining neutral in World War II, Swiss army knives, the Alps, and Roger Federer. But not for its nocturnal warmth! We needed shelter for the night, or it was pretty certain we'd all get pneumonia or

frostbite. My friend Sean scoped out a bench along the street and figured it would be the perfect place to grab 40 winks. He pointed to
the bench, which was surrounded by snow, and hooted, "Ram in the
thicket!"

"No, Sean," I said. "That is *not* a ram in the thicket."

The night was diamond studded and blue the color of ice on a polar
bear's back, but it was *freezing*.

We wandered into the only hotel we still hadn't investigated in hopes
of finding a better place than that unwelcoming bench, but we could
see that it was way too fancy for our budget. Nine Americans in the
middle of the night crowded into the lobby, along with all our camera
gear. I plopped down on a couch, mourning in despair that we couldn't
scrounge up enough money to pay for rooms. I just stared at the wall,
my head down, feeling a little depressed and very discouraged.

Then I looked up, and there were rams everywhere! We were surrounded by them—there was a ram's head mounted on the wall, a
logo of a ram on the desk, and even the business cards of the hotel had a
ram as part of the design. Rams, rams, rams everywhere! Coincidence?
I think not. Rams as white as moonlight on snow surrounded us.

I sprang from the couch. "Guys! The Spirit is about to do something.
He is on the move. There are rams everywhere! Provision! Provision is
coming!"

The hotel manager behind the desk was obviously drunk, and so my
friend Madison asked aloud, "This hotel is too expensive for us. Can
we all just stay at your house?"

Maybe it's different in Switzerland, but in America you can't just show
up for your work as a night manager completely hammered.

He gave a tipsy shrug and muttered, "Okay."

The nine of us squeezed into his apartment overlooking the Matterhorn. It was, well, cozy. When the manager woke up and sobered up, he looked at the nine American strangers sharing his room and didn't know who, in the name of all that is wonderful, we were. He asked us to kindly leave.

Well-rested, warmed-up, and ready for the day after a good night's sleep, we stepped out of his apartment into a brisk morning. I leaned over to Sean and said, "Now *that*, Sean, was a ram in the thicket!"

((((( )))))

God can use even a drunken hotel manager to accomplish His purposes of provision.

Jehovah Jireh is, to use my own theological term, *awesometastic*.

When you buy a new car, have you ever noticed that you see cars all over the place just like yours? You never noticed them before, but now you do. Well, now I notice rams everywhere! I recently saw a rainbow ram statue in the Palm Springs airport and a less colorful one in a Nevada airport. I took photos of them and texted them to my companions on our European Extravaganza as a reminder of the God who says, "Providing is My middle name!"

Even when you're in the cold and feel lost, dear reader, remember that provision is on the way!

Let's ride the wild rams with our friends on the highest mountain peaks until Kingdom come.

THE INTERIORITY
COMPLEX

Sigmund Freud thought a person's psychological constitution was driven by infantile sexuality. Victor Frankl thought the primary psychological quest was the search for meaning. Carl Jung suggested that we needed to examine our dreams to understand ourselves. And Alfred Adler coined the phrase "inferiority complex" in the belief that how we thought about ourselves was of critical concern for our psychological health. They were all trying to make sense of our psychological ailments. As I wrote in *Optimisfits*, I think Victor Frankl comes closest to getting it right.[1] But in this chapter, I'd like to ponder the thoughts of Alfred Adler.

At the turn of the twentieth century, Adler put forward an interesting theory called "compensation." When he studied a large group of art students, he found that 70 percent of them had optical anomalies.[2] He also noted that two of the greatest composers in history, Mozart and Beethoven, had degenerative conditions in their ears.[3] He noted a similar pattern in all kinds of areas—those with weaknesses they had to overcome went on to be highly successful in their field of endeavor. You'd think that a problem seeing would be an insurmountable setback for painters, or a problem hearing one for composers. But Adler demonstrated that what we assume to be our disadvantages frequently prove to be our advantages in the end because we learn to compensate for our lack. They force us to dig deep to cultivate compensatory abilities that would otherwise have lain dormant.

Birth defects, illness, poverty, and negative circumstances often prove to be a springboard to success!

This "discovery" is something that Jesus was teaching all along: It is in our weakness that we find strength.

Paul wrote, "When I am weak, then I am strong" (2 Corinthians 12:10). He gloried in his weakness.

The prophet Joel had written many years earlier: "Let the weak say, I am strong" (Joel 3:10 KJV).

In other words, your *oddities* are your *commodities*, as His strength is made perfect in your weakness.

((((( )))))

Don't live in fear of your negative circumstances or inborn disadvantages, because God is ready to redeem them. To make something beautiful from them.

Adler's data rings psychic cherries with me on a visceral level. My own life experiences might easily have given me an inferiority complex, but the Holy Spirit wants to work on the inside so that I have an *interiority complex*. The struggles of my life, and the depression that always nipped at my heels, might have predisposed me to have a gloomy view of the world. But when God freed me from my melancholia, working from the inside out, I found a new vision: saving the world from the ravages of depression. I could speak from experience. I'm not so much saying to those who will listen, "hear my words," as I'm saying, "touch my wounds." My *pains* have become the *birth pangs* of the Hope Generation.

I decided it was my job to stand at the gates of Hades and redirect traffic.

((((( )))))

Someone once said to me in a dismissive tone, "Depressed people are weak."

My first response was to think that this line of thinking is one of the reasons why depression and suicide have reached such levels in our time. People struggling don't need condemnation or shame. They need compassion.

And then I thought, *Truth is, we are all weak.* Everyone struggles with all kinds of different issues. If depression isn't one of your struggles, I'm happy for you.

Let's just admit that we *all* have an Adlerian inferiority complex. Sometimes, deep down, we all feel like imposters—not as good, put together, or happy as people think we are. We are looking over our shoulder to see who might be competing with us. We compare ourselves with others on social media.

Let's just admit that all of us are weak. For in that admission, I've found, we can find our strength—God's strength. Then He can take our brokenness and make it into something beautiful.

So, change your mind about your disadvantages and insecurities. Stare them down and move forward anyway.

As Robert Schuller said, "Let your hopes, not your hurts, shape your future."

CUE THE MIC DROP

People are not your dictionary, so don't let them define you.

Other people might put us down, but they cannot take us down.

Neuroscience is now telling us that negativity sticks to the brain like Velcro, but, unfortunately, good news slips off the brain like eggs in a nonstick pan.[1] That's why, when nine people compliment your Instagram post and only one person says something mean about it, you can't stop thinking about the one negative comment. That's how your psychological constitution works. To assimilate good news, you need to take 15 seconds to meditate on it so that it becomes sticky. When it comes to our gray cells, neuropathways, and our general cranial package, it just takes longer to process encouragement.

So instead of being subsumed by the oppression of negative social media, we should meditate on what is lovely and noble and true, as embedded in the promises of God.

Take 15 seconds to let this soak in:

Here is what God thinks of you. You are His masterpiece, His *poiema* (His poem). You are *imago Dei*, an image bearer of the Divine. You are a temple of the Holy Spirit, hosting the very presence of God. You are seated in heavenly places—not in the nosebleed section. You have a reserved box seat with Jesus on His throne. You are a king. You are a priest, speaking to God for the people and speaking to the people for God. You are fearfully and wonderfully made. You are a jewel. You are a pearl of great price. You are the apple of His eye.

Not bad, eh?

When you feel crummy about yourself, keep these truths in mind. These are the things that the Bible says you are.

You are ridiculously, absurdly, passionately loved.

This ain't the blues. This is good news.

(((( ))))

When Jesus went to celebrate the Passover as a 12-year-old kid, He spent His time debating with the scribes and the scholars in the temple. History tells us that the very same year the temple was profaned. When they opened the doors of the temple one morning, they found the bones of dead men scattered all over the whole place. Josephus, the historian who recounts this story, tells us that it was likely done by Samaritans to spite their Jewish brothers.[2] But is it possible something bigger was going on? That it was a sign from God that the temple services would soon be replaced by the words of the Lord of Heaven, the 12-year-old whose own body would be sacrificed to replace the whole system? Jesus said His body was a temple that would be destroyed, but that He would raise it up on the third day.

The God of hope was bringing hope as a replacement for religion.

(((( ))))

Though the source escapes me, years ago it caused my brain to reel when I learned that, according to scientists who work with brain scans, one of the chief benefits of religious faith is that it creates a sense of identity. Once we know who the Lord is, we will know who we are. That's why Jesus gave Peter a new identity during their conversation at Caesarea Philippi. They were in a town loaded with religious history. On the hillside was a gleaming marble temple devoted to the godhood of Caesar. There was a cave believed to be the birthplace of Pan, the Greek god of nature. There was a spring where water flowed which was believed to be the source of the Jordan River, an archetypal centerpiece of Judaism. And this was also once a great center for the worship of Baal.

Against that backdrop—a backdrop of the major world religions— Jesus asked His followers, "Who do you say that I am?"

Peter gave the right answer: "You are the Christ" (Matthew 16:15-16, Mark 8:29; Luke 9:20 NASB).

So in response, Jesus gave him a new identity right then and there. He told Him that He would now be called "the rock" (Matthew 16:18) He changed from Simon (which means "shifting sand") to Peter, the Rock!

((((( )))))

How you believe God thinks about you will have a powerful effect on how you see God. What you think about Him is the most important thing about you, because research shows that your attitudes will mirror your theology. If you identify the Lord as a cruel despot, always prepared to squash you for displeasing Him, you'll be a judgmental grumpy Gus. But if you see him as the apostle Paul did—as the God of Hope—it'll turn you into a hope dealer. And hope, my friend, is dope.

You are not just a carbon footprint taking up space. You are a force to be reckoned with.

You are not a collection of protons. You are a pronoun.

You are not an orphan. You are a child of the Most High.

Drop the mic.

LIONS AND BUTTERFLIES

I speak for a living. I'm always on the move, traveling around the country (and sometimes overseas) to speak with audiences of people. And I love it.

But that doesn't mean it doesn't make me nervous. They say public speaking is one of most people's greatest fears. Everyone is scared that when they stand up in front of a group of people they'll make a fool of themselves. (Which I have probably done more times than I care to admit!)

Sometimes, though, you have to take a risk.

Here's the deal. I have learned to love, love, love taking the risk.

To quote Jean-Paul Sartre, "To know what your life is worth, you have to risk it once in a while." Better to die doing what you love than to live doing nothing at all. "Only those who will risk going too far can possibly find out how far one *can* go," T.S. Eliot said. These are the trailblazers, the heroes.

The Bible says, "The righteous are as bold as a lion" (Proverbs 28:1).

((((( )))))

I've been giving talks in public since I was in third grade. In recent years I have spoken on average ten times a week. With all that experience, the truth is I still get keyed up before I speak—my heart thumps like a bass drum, my pulse quickens, and my mind races. I've learned, though, to use this adrenaline to my advantage. And I love the passion that rises alongside the fear.

As Rob Bell says,

> *Nerves are God's gift to you, reminding you that your life is not passing you by.*
>
> Make friends with the butterflies.
>
> Welcome them when they come,
>
> revel in them,
>
> enjoy them,
>
> and if they go away, do whatever it takes to put yourself in a position where they return.
>
> Better to have a stomach full of butterflies than to feel like your life is passing you by.[1]

You may not be a public speaker like me, but I know you have something in your life that you love to do but that terrifies you. Something that increases your pulse rate, makes your hands sweat, and scares you half to death. Well, good. Pursue that. Don't be afraid of it.

Chesterton told us to "desire life like water and yet drink death like wine."[2] That, in the words of Tennyson, is "the temper of heroic hearts."[3]

Do the thing you fear, and remember you don't have to do it alone. You'll never be less lonely than when you are alone with God. When my primary stage is a wooden floor where I kneel before that audience of One, then an audience of thousands is not such a big deal. I can be a roaring lion because I know the Lion of Judah. He is with me in whatever might frighten me. So, I will follow Aslan—further up and further in.

Because He's got this…then I've got this!

NO, YOU'RE
NOT DEPRESSED

News bulletin: We are officially the most depressed generation in history. At least that is what we are being told by the experts.

So, I'm wondering who interviewed the fourteenth-century Burgundians, for example, to make sure we are safe in that assumption.

Okay, so it isn't too hard to believe this is true if you look around at how a lot of people seem to be feeling. The emotional gloom seems to be spreading. Lots of people are flirting with darkness. But is this something we have to just quietly accept? No.

Cue the Hope Generators, who know this fact…and defy it.

Via neuroplasticity, we are set upon reshaping the collective consciousness of our generation by telling our generation about the truth that sets us free. And if your truth isn't setting you free, then it isn't really the truth!

$((((\ ))))$

You might not be feeling your best right now, but that isn't the whole story.

Here is the truth about you:

You are not stuck being a victim of depression. No way. You are free. You are loved. God loved you so much that He came down from heaven to make a place for Himself within you—a cozy home for His love to dwell inside the deepest part of your being. If heaven is His home, and He chose to relocate inside of you, you must be pretty special.

You and I are containers for the Creator, with divinity indwelling us. We are like the Old Testament Holy of Holies; a place where God abides.

We carry the God of hope around in our earthsuits.

When you understand that God finds you to be a worthy home for Himself, you should feel the wonder bubbling up inside you. If you really comprehend this truth, you should experience the Great Mystery, which has been defined as the lump you feel in your throat when you shudder at wonder. The jaded cynicism of postmodernism will lose its credibility in the light of this knowledge and of the grandness humming in your heart.

He is the Ground of Being, the Prime Mover, the Initial Singularity of Infinite Density, the Quantum Reality, the Oz Behind the Curtain, and the Origin from which flamingoes spring. And He chooses to live in you!

You host His presence.

So, how can you think it's your destiny to be hopeless when your blood cells carry the very life of God and Divine presence courses through your veins?

Kindly reconsider, my friend.

(((( ))))

The problem is, this truth is inconceivable if you don't really understand who God is.

A lot of people think God is a distant, all-powerful parental figure who has set impossible standards and made unbearable demands upon us. They don't think they can be chill with the Almighty and besties with the Creator. They consider themselves utterly unworthy to be a house for God. They don't believe God really loves and adores them.

Our view of God is often predicated upon our cultural surroundings and personal experiences because culture has a way of eating ideology for lunch. In Germany, God looks like a police officer. In Switzerland, like a banker. In America, like a capitalist businessman. And, as the book *Fight Club* suggests, maybe every son models his image of God on his earthly dad…which is bad news for a lot of orphans.[1]

But none of these things captures who God really is.

God, says the Bible, is love.

No policy, campaign, set of daddy issues, or extenuating circumstances will ever change that.

We must always beware of understanding God through the lens of our childhood experiences at home, our political persuasions, our philosophical convictions, or even our religious traditions. The real God simply doesn't fit into any of these boxes. Nor does He fit into our tidy boxes of pious rules and regulations and legalism. A lot of religious people are afraid of the untamed God of love, so they work especially hard to box Him into something that fits more comfortably with what they think to be true.

But trying to put God in a box is like putting Him into a tomb. Give Him three days and He'll bust out.

Nothing but taillights…

So, let God love you into freedom.

You may struggle with depression now and then, but you don't have to live there.

The Bible says you have a "sound mind" (1 Timothy 1:7 KJV). It doesn't say you have a sick mind. Which of these you believe will affect the way you live. Embrace the truth and leave depression behind.

DANCE IN DEFIANCE
OF THE DARK

Well, friends near and far, I hope reading my words in this book has helped you find a little bit of peace and a lotta bit of hope, and that it might have even helped a few readers to step back from the brink. You can choose a different way of living.

It's easy to romanticize suicide, to see it as somehow heroic. After all, it has claimed the life of many a genius, from Seneca to Sylvia Plath. The dark void at the end of your story can seem like a perfectly fine way to draw down the curtain.

Kurt Cobain, a rock and roll icon who donned a cardigan and unleashed a guttural growl of passion, was one whose music stood as a witness against the dominant, hair spray, hard-metal music. He chose the darkness. He wrote his suicide note to his imaginary childhood friend, Boddah. Perhaps this heartthrob of Gen X was thinking of the words Neil Young sang about Johnny Rotten of the Sex Pistols: "Better to burn out than to fade away." And so he "burned out" at his own hands and added his name to the roster of the young who killed themselves, alongside Ernest Hemingway, David Foster Wallace, and Robin Williams.

When I flirted with darkness, I was under the same sort of spell, thinking it was a poetic way to announce my displeasure with what life had to offer me. After all, the great metaphysician Albert Camus identified the most-important philosophical question of the twentieth century when he asked, "Should we kill ourselves?" If life is worth living, then fine, we won't kill ourselves. But if it proves to be more of a torment than a pleasure…well then, we might as well just skip right to the end. We are going to die anyway, so we might as well change the date.

((((( )))))

I spent some time out on that ledge, flirting with darkness and looking for a way out. Only later did I learn that my panic attacks, easily triggered anxiety, and debilitating depression were something that a counselor would eventually diagnose as complex PTSD.

Before that, I thought sadness and hopelessness were just the way of the world. The great novelist William Styron, author of such modern classics as *Sophie's Choice*, wrote a book about his personal struggle against depression. He called it *Darkness Visible*. He described depression as a bank of fog that rolled in every morning. Dark. Poisonous. I think he was exactly right. Suicide isn't a romantic or poetic option. It's a surrender to darkness.

I came to understand the error of the seductive power that lured me to the edge, and the false reasoning that suggested that suicide was a valid choice. So, I stepped back from that ledge.

If you are hanging out on the ledge, you can step back too.

Right now.

((((( )))))

We've kind of normalized suicide in our modern culture. We've been sold a bill of goods: the lie that it is a perfectly good option. The result is that in America, suicides are more prevalent than homicides. Hearing about someone killing themselves just isn't as shocking as it used to be. In fact, some suggest, suicide might even be considered beautiful or normal.

This isn't true. It's a tragic deception that has claimed too many lives. I am counting on this generation to be the one that decides we are going to stand up against this epidemic. Depression is a worthy foe. So we will take up the weapons found in the arsenal of this book, and we will be happy warriors, joyful soldiers, and heroic stoics. The dark lord will meet his end. We are going to show the world that hope is a better producer of meaning and happiness and purpose than despair can ever be. We are going to debunk the lie that creativity and advancement only come from tortured souls.

Why, we ask, can't genius arise from joy and hope instead of depression?

((((( )))))

This is my battle, and it's a war I'm winning. Every time the enemy shoves me down to the bottom, I can climb back out of the hole. I can take hold of the heavenly Hand that reaches down to me even in my darkest moments.

I'm sure I'll still have moments when I want to sob and hyperventilate and lay supine on the bathroom floor, convinced I will never be happy again. I'll complain and throw stuff at the wall and wail in rage. I'll probably have mornings when I don't even want to get out of bed.

But those moments are the *exception*. And these things shall pass. With God's help I'm going to be a spiritual SEAL and claw my way out of the pit when I find myself there.

The reason blockbuster films like *The Avengers* break box office records is because, like the Hulk and Captain America, we too are in a war. We relate to battle scenes in movies because we fight our own every day. Each of us must decide not to surrender to that seductive darkness and continue to fight on.

I have fought my way out of the pit more than once. You can too. It may not be easy, but it's worth the effort.

This I know for sure. We are in a conflict of epic proportions. Each of us is called to battle. Let us do deeds of daring, feats in the field, acts for the annals, and exploits worthy of remembrance.

And let us love every moment of the journey.

So, what are you going to do?

Flirt with darkness?

Or dance with light?

(((( ))))

The amazing thing about joggers is that they run even when there is no fire or no dog chasing them.

Marathons are even more amazing. A marathon is a 26-mile run, and its name comes from an event in the history of ancient Greece. After a series of crushing defeats at the hands of the Persians, things looked bad for the Greeks. They were outnumbered four to one, but miraculously, they pulled off a victory.

Because of the potential of an attack coming from ships at sea, news of their victory had to be relayed to Athens. The Greeks summoned a soldier named Pheidippides, who had fought all day, and told him to run from Marathon to Athens with the news. The distance between those two cities—you guessed it—was 26 miles. He ran and ran and ran, no doubt snorting like a warthog. When he reached Athens, utterly exhausted, he shouted "Victory!" and then he dropped down dead.

We will win our battle against depression. Only after we've declared, "Victory"—and not one second sooner—will we allow ourselves to drop down dead.

NOTES

Why I Wrote This Book

1. John Mark Comer, *Garden City* (Grand Rapids, MI: Zondervan, 2017), 40.

Chapter 2. Squirt Gun Drive-bys and Funeral Directors

1. C.S. Lewis, *A Grief Observed* (New York: HarperOne, 1994), 69.

2. William Barclay, *The New Daily Study Bible: The Gospel of Luke* (Louisville, KY: Westminster John Knox Press, 2001), 231.

3. Ibid.

4. Algernon Charles Swinburne, "Hymn to Prosperpine (After the Proclamation in Rome of the Christian Faith)," *Laus Veneris: And Other Poems and Ballads* (New York: Carleton, 1867), 77.

5. Jonathan Edwards, *Sinners in the Hands of an Angry God: A Sermon* (Edinburgh: T. Lumisden and J. Robertson, 1745).

Chapter 4. Facing the Dark Lord

1. Adapted from Charles E. Cowman, Mrs., L.B.E. Cowman, *Streams in the Desert* (Grand Rapids, MI: Zondervan, 2006), 69.

2. Cowman, *Streams in the Desert*, 70.

Chapter 6. There Will Be Blood in the Battle

1. Mandy Oaklander, "How to Bounce Back," *Special Times Edition: The Science of Happiness* (eBook, Time Incorporated Books, 2016), https://www.google.com/books/edition/TIME_The_Science _of_Happiness/7CWiDAAAQBAJ?hl=en&gbpv=0.

Chapter 7. Weapon #1: Prayer Walks

1. James A. Blumenthal et al., "Effects of Exercise Training on Older Patients with Major Depression," *Arch Intern Med* 159, no. 19 (October 25, 1999), 2349–56, doi: 10.1001/archinte.159.19.2349.

2. Cindy Trimm, *Goodbye, Yesterday!* (Lake Mary, FL: Charisma House, 2020), 12.

3. Kirk I. Erickson, "Exercise Training Increases Size of Hippocampus and Improves Memory," *Proceedings of the National Academy of Sciences* 108, no. 7 (February 2011), 3017–22, doi: 10.1073/pnas.1015950108.

4. Joyce Meyer, *Me and My Big Mouth! Your Answer Is Right Under Your Nose* (New York: FaithWords, 2008), 36.

5. Mike McHargue, *Finding God in the Waves* (New York: Convergent Books, 2016), 176.

6. Henry Baker Tristram, *The Natural History of the Bible* (London: Society for Promoting Christian Knowledge, 1883), 221.

Chapter 8. Weapon #2: Scripture Scholar Scuba Gear

1. This trinity of time, space, and matter was first noted in Nathan R. Wood's *The Secret of the Universe: God, Man, and Matter* (Grand Rapids, MI: W.B. Eerdmans Publishers, 1959).

2. The link between grief and separation anxiety was first noted in John Bowlby's *Separation: Anxiety and Anger* (New York: Basic Books, 1976).

3. Bjorn Carey, "Dolphins Name Themselves," Live Science, May 8, 2006, https://www.livescience.com/748-dolphins.html.

Chapter 9. Weapon #3: The Magic Number of Greatness

1. Malcolm Gladwell, *Outliers: The Story of Success* (New York: Little, Brown and Company, 2008), 35.

2. Colin Robertson, "The True Secret Behind Mozart's Genius," Willpowered, December 15, 2015, http://www.willpowered.co/learn/true-secret-mozart.

3. Jane McGonigal, "Video Games: An Hour A Day Is Key To Success In Life," HuffPost, July28, 2011, https://www.huffpost.com/entry/video-games_b_823208.

4. J.S. Ross, "The Eighteenth Century Pentecost," *Methodist Magazine and Review*, Volume LVIII (Toronto: William Briggs Methodist Publishing House, July–December 1903), 442.

5. John Wesley, *The Works of the Rev. John Wesley: In Ten Volumes*, Volume IV (New York: Harper, 1826), 175.

6. "5 Must-Read Stories from 49ers Legends Steve Young and Jerry Rice," 49ers.com, September 1, 2016, www.49ers.com/news/5-must-read-stories-from-49ers-legends-steve-young-and-jerry-rice-17597342.

Chapter 10. Weapon #4: Endorphins, Anyone?

1. Kristen Domonell, "Why endorphins (and exercise) make you happy," CNN, January 13, 2016, https://www.cnn.com/2016/01/13/health/endorphins-exercise-cause-happiness/index.html.

Chapter 12. Weapon #6: Own Your Oddness

1. http://penelope.uchicago.edu/Thayer/E/Roman/Texts/Plutarch/Lives/Caesar*.html.

2. David Blatner, *Spectrums: Our Mind-Boggling Universe from Infinitesimal to Infinity* (New York: Bloomsbury, 2012), 20.

3. "How many hairs are there on the human head?" Bauman Medical, February 12, 2014, https://www.baumanmedical.com/qa/many-hairs-human-head.

4. Jim Carrey, "What It All Means: One of the Most Eye Opening Speeches," YouTube, November 4, 2017, https://www.youtube.com/watch?v=wTblbYqQQag.

5. Sarah Pruitt, "The First Left-handed President Was Ambidextrous and Multilingual," History, August 13, 2018, https://www.history.com/news/first-left-handed-president-ambidextrous-multilingual.

Chapter 13. Weapon #7: Friendventures

1. Amy Morin, "Loneliness Is as Lethal as Smoking 15 Cigarettes Per Day. Here's What You Can Do About It," Inc.com, June 18, 2018, https://www.inc.com/amy-morin/americas-loneliness -epidemic-is-more-lethal-than-smoking-heres-what-you-can-do-to-combat-isolation.html.

Chapter 14. Weapon #8: Heaven

1. William Barclay, *The New Daily Study Bible: The Letters of James and Peter* (Louisville, KY: Westminster John Knox Press, 2003), 316.

Chapter 15. Weapon #9: El Roi

1. Naomi I. Eisenberger, Matthew D. Lieberman, and Kipling D. Williams, "Does Rejection Hurt? An fMRI Study of Social Exclusion," Science 302, no. 5643 (October 10, 2003), 290–92, doi: 10.1126/science.1089134.

2. Cornelius Tacitus, "Signs and Wonders," ourcivilization.com, http://www.ourcivilisation.com /smartboard/shop/tacitusc/histries/chap17.htm.

3. Michael Waters, "The Public Shaming of England's First Umbrella User," Atlas Obscura, July 27, 2016, https://www.atlasobscura.com/articles/the-public-shaming-of-englands-first-umbrella-user.

4. A.G. McKenzie, "Another Look at Religious Objections to Obstetric Anaesthesia," International Journal of Obstetric Anesthesia 27 (August 2016), 62–65, doi: 10.1016/j.ijoa.2016.05.003.

5. Luke 4:40-41; 5:12-13; 5:17-25; 6:6-10; 7:1-10; 7:11-15; 8:26-33; 8:41-55; 9:37-43; 13:11-13; 17:11-19; 18:35-43; 22:50-51.

6. "The Most Important Lesson from 83,000 Brain Scans: Daniel Amen," New World Artificial Intelligence, March 27, 2020, https://www.newworldai.com/the-most-important-lesson-from-83 -000-brain-scans-daniel-amen/.

Chapter 17. Dreamality

1. Remez Sasson, "How Many Thoughts Does Your Mind Think in One Hour?" Success Consciousness, https://www.successconsciousness.com/blog/inner-peace/how-many-thoughts-does-your -mind-think-in-one-hour/.

2. 1 Corinthians 15:54; 1 Samuel 17:47; Isaiah 42:13; Romans 8:31; Isaiah 54:17.

3. T.E. Lawrence, *Seven Pillars of Wisdom* (Knoxville, TN: Wordsworth Classics, 1997), 7.

Chapter 18. Of Tolkien, Lewis, and the Phrygian Legend

1. "War Made C.S. Lewis," War Is Boring, October 9, 2014, https://medium.com/war-is-boring /war-made-c-s-lewis-83d90682f4e1.

2. C.S. Lewis, *Surprised by Joy* (New York: Harcourt Brace, 1955), 195-196.

Chapter 19. Theology and Thief-ology

1. Elizabeth Howell, "How Man Stars Are in the Milky Way?" Space, March 30, 2018, https://www .space.com/25959-how-many-stars-are-in-the-milky-way.html.

2. "Hexapoda—The Insects," Wildlife Journal Junior, https://nhpbs.org/wild/hexapoda.asp.

3. Joe Skogmo, "An Aggressive Shepherd—Psalm 23," pastorjoeskogmo, March 31, 2014, https://pastor joeskogmo.wordpress.com/2014/03/31/an-aggressive-shepherd-psalm-23.

Chapter 20. Brain Power!

1. "Brain Neurons & Synapses," The Human Memory, September 27, 2019, https://human-memory .net/brain-neurons-synapses/.

2. "How Much Energy Does the Brain Use?" BrainFacts.org, February 1, 2019, https://www.brainfacts .org/brain-anatomy-and-function/anatomy/2019/how-much-energy-does-the-brain-use-020119.

3. Paul Reber, "What Is the Memory of the Human Brain?" Scientific American, May 1, 2010, https:// www.scientificamerican.com/article/what-is-the-memory-capacity/.

4. Barbara Bradley Hagerty, "Prayer May Reshape Your Brain…And Your Reality," NPR, May 20, 2009, https://www.npr.org/templates/story/story.php?storyId=104310443.

Chapter 22. The Chapter That Starts with a Lousy Joke

1. Sally C. Curtin and Melonie Heron, "Death Rates Due to Suicide and Homicide Among Persons Aged 10–24: United States, 2000–2017," NCHS Data Brief, no. 352, October 2019, www.cdc.gov /nchs/products/databriefs/db352.htm.

Chapter 23. The Thanksliving Gratitude Attitude

1. Joel Wong, Joshua Brown, "How Gratitude Changes You and Your Brain," Greater Good, June 6, 2017, https://greatergood.berkeley.edu/article/item/how_gratitude_changes_you_and_your_brain.

2. Gyles Brandreth, *The Joy of Lex: How to Have Fun with 860,341,500 Words* (London, Guild Publishing, 1987).

Chapter 24. The Eneffable Tetragrammaton

1. Rob Bell, *NOOMA: Breathe* (Grand Rapids, MI: Zondervan, 2006), DVD.

Chapter 27. Don't Drink the Boos

1. Ben Courson, *Optimisfits* (Eugene, OR: Harvest House Publishers, 2019), 101-102.

Chapter 29. Forget the Mud

1. Charles Spurgeon, "Who Found It Out?" from *Metropolitan Tabernacle Pulpit*, Volume 32, June 6, 1886, www.spurgeon.org/resource-library/sermons/who-found-it-out.

Chapter 30. Surfing the Wonders

1. Rob Bell, *What We Talk About When We Talk About God* (New York: HarperOne, 2014), 27-28.

2. G.K. Chesterton, *On Lying in Bed and Other Essays* (Calgary, AB: Bayeux Arts, 2000), 71.

3. Megan Garber, "How Many Stars Are There in the Sky?" The Atlantic, November 19, 2013, www .theatlantic.com/technology/archive/2013/11/how-many-stars-are-there-in-the-sky/281641.

4. Charles Spurgeon, "August 22," Morning and Evening (Peabody, MA: Hendrickson Publishers, 1991), 471.

Chapter 33. When Holidays Are Hard

1. Anna Greenberg and Jennifer Berktold, "Holiday Stress," American Pscyhologian Association Press Release, December 12, 2006, 4–5, www.apa.org/news/press/releases/2006/12/holiday-stress .pdf.

2. Christian Smith and Melinda Lundquist Denton, *Soul Searching: The Religious and Spiritual Lives of American Teenagers* (New York: Oxford University Press, 2005), 162.

Chapter 34. Welcome to Hogwarts, You Muggles

1. Smadar Naoz, "The Milky Way may have two supermassive black holes," Astronomy, December 12, 2019, https://astronomy.com/news/2019/12/the-milky-way-may-have-two-supermassive-black-holes.

2. Fraser Cain, "How Many Earths Can Fit in the Sun?" Universe Today, https://www.universetoday.com/65356/how-many-earths-can-fit-in-the-sun/amp/.

3. "Io Overview," https://solarsystem.nasa.gov/moons/jupiter-moons/io/overview/.

4. Neil deGrasse Tyson, *Death by Black Hole* (New York: W. W. Norton & Co., 2007), 35.

5. "How big does a meteor have to be to make it to the ground?" Science, https://science.howstuffworks.com/question486.htm.

6. "Rain Facts for Kids," Science Kids, https://www.sciencekids.co.nz/sciencefacts/weather/rain.html.

7. Rob Bell, *What We Talk About When We Talk About God* ((New York: HarperOne, 2014), 24.

Chapter 39. The Interiority Complex

1. Ben Courson, *Optimisfits* (Eugene, OR: Harvest House Publishers, 2019), 145-147.

2. Alfred Adler, *Study of Organ Inferiority and Its Psychical Compensation: A Contribution to Clinical Medicine*, trans. Smith Ely Jelliffe (New York: The Nervous and Mental Disease Publishing Company, 1917), 61.

3. Ibid., 28.

Chapter 40. Cue the Mic Drop

1. Rick Hanson, "Taking In the Good," Psychology Today, February 5, 2010, https://www.psychologytoday.com/us/blog/your-wise-brain/201002/taking-in-the-good.

2. "Judean-Samaritan Feud," virtualreligion.net, # 60, https://virtualreligion.net/iho/samaria.html.

Chapter 41. Lions and Butterflies

1. Rob Bell, *How to Be Here: A Guide to Creating a Life Worth Living* (New York: HarperOne, 2017), 106.

2. G.K. Chesterton, *Wit and Wisdom of G.K. Chesterton* (New York: Dodd, Mead and Company, 1911), 2.

3. Alfred Tennyson, *Ulysses and Columbus* (London: Macmillan and Co., 1913), 15.

Chapter 42: No, You're Not Depressed

1. Chuck Palahniuk, *Fight Club* (New York: W.W. Norton & Co., 1996), 186.

ACKNOWLEDGMENTS

In an effort to avoid anything akin to an Oscar speech, I'll try to keep the acknowledgments short. After all, the mind can only absorb what the seat can endure. All bloviating aside, I must say that my buttons are bursting with pride for each person involved in this project. I stand in the debt of many contributors who helped contour *Flirting with Darkness* into what it is today. That list includes, but is not limited, to:

Terry Glaspey, an award-winning author in his own right who doubles as our brilliant Editor-in-Chief. You've shown me a portal through the wardrobe, old friend. To the renaissance we go! Huzzah!

Kim Moore for being your friendly neighborhood Chief of the Grammar Police. Love ya, Kim!

Vice President Sherrie Slopianka for pouring oodles of funds, time, and gentle loving care into all my projects.

President Bob Hawkins for running literal and metaphorical marathons. Bob, you get a gold medal for how you've RUN this publishing company. Say it with me now: "Victory!"

Shannon Hartley and the PR team for being marketing wizards.

Faceout for crafting a mesmerizing cover.

And all the fantastical people at Harvest House!

Thanks a million to my *Hope Generation* TV and radio family back home: John Swenson, The Bates Boys: Dylan, Jeff, and Taylor; Deb Steffy; Jereme Dittmer; and Mombo Courson for spreading this message and for building outposts of sacred optimism all over the world.

My friends and fam: sloppy bear hugs for one and all!

And lastly, to you, for making it to the end of the book. Woo to the hoo! May the hope be with you!

ABOUT THE AUTHOR

Ben Courson is an international speaker, bestselling author, TV and radio personality, and senior pastor of Applegate Christian Fellowship. He has been featured on Fox, Hallmark Channel, TBN, ABC Family, and other mainstream media outlets. His TV show, *Hope Generation with Ben Courson*, is broadcast in 180 countries, and his radio show airs on more than 400 stations nationally. Ben travels the globe speaking of God's hope and igniting revival in the hearts of his listeners.

Stemming from his own bout with suicide and depression, Ben founded *Hope Generation*, aiming to help those struggling with depression and suicidal thoughts as well as those who have lost hope and meaning amid their success. He sincerely shares his own struggles of heartbreak, being diagnosed with complex PTSD, and the devastating losses of his brother and sister. Ben is shouting about the God of hope from the mountaintops to help people rise out of despair.

Ben's high energy, humor, and deep biblical understanding have impacted people from all walks of life. As a social media influencer, he has reached millions of YouTube viewers who have tuned in to watch and listen to *Hope Generation*. Ben is infiltrating old and new media alike and spreading God's message of hope like fire.

Hope Generation is a play on words that suggests both a personal and collective appeal: Generating hope in God and building a generation of hope. That is the mission of *Hope Generation*.

BIBLE CREDITS

OPTI MIS FITS

IGNITING A FIERCE REBELLION

AGAINST HOPELESSNESS

BEN COURSON

FOUNDER OF HOPE GENERATION

"Ben Courson is a vital voice for this generation." —**Rich Wilkerson Jr.**

"This book will give you clear and simple direction to unleash hope, faith, and optimism in your life as you become an Optimisfit!" —**Levi Lusko**

Op•ti•mis•fit, n: a nonconformist, an adventurer, a person who lives with wild abandon, childlike wonder, and unapologetic optimism.

You were never meant to fit in. You were *made* to stand out.

With passion, purpose, a large dose of humor, and a wild sense of wonder, *Optimisfits* offers a road map for a better way to live. It's calling you to seize your status as an outsider and wage a fierce rebellion against the hopelessness of the world by living out an intensely optimistic approach to every day.

Ben Courson and a band of misfits invite you to join them on an epic adventure with God and with the Squad.

#hopeisdope! And it's time to spread it like fire. Are you ready to make a *real* difference and ignite the world? Join the Optimisfits and see sparks fly!

To learn more about Harvest House books and
to read sample chapters, visit our website:

www.harvesthousepublishers.com

HARVEST HOUSE PUBLISHERS
EUGENE, OREGON